Turner, Frederick.
Remembering song

DATE DUE

APR. 14, 1989 RET			

A FINE WILL BE CHARGED FOR
EACH OVERDUE BOOK AT THE
RATE OF 10 CENTS PER DAY.

DEMCO

REMEMBERING SONG

Frederick Turner

REMEMBERING SONG

Encounters with the
New Orleans Jazz Tradition

THE VIKING PRESS · NEW YORK

For Elise:
the only song I know

LIBRARY OF CONGRESS CATALOGING IN PUBLICATION DATA
Turner, Frederick.
  Remembering song.
  1. Jazz music—Louisiana—New Orleans.
2. Afro-American music—Louisiana—New Orleans—
History and criticism. I. Title.
ML3508.T87   785.42'09763'35   81-16470
ISBN 0-670-59375-3   AACR2

"A Music of the Streets" appeared originally in *Massachusetts Review,* and "A History of 'Hot' " in *American Heritage,* in different form.

Printed in the United States of America
Set in Video Baskerville

No matter what he's playing,
it's the long song that started
back there in the South.
It's the remembering song.
There's so much to remember.
—SIDNEY BECHET

Preface

It is best to define one's terms at the outset in the attempt to avoid misunderstanding, disappointment, or charges of false advertising.

This is not a "jazz book." Jazz books are usually written for "aficionados"—a word which in our language is reserved for devotees of bullfighting and jazz, both presumably odd passions. Jazz books assume a deep familiarity with the history of jazz and thus an interest in such details as lines of stylistic descent, changes in band personnel, the contents of famous solos, recording sessions, discography, and bibliography. *Remembering Song*, on the other hand, is a book about a particular aspect of American cultural history, the folk origins and subsequent development of a musical tradition. It assumes on the part of readers a general interest in the national life as well as some interest in seeing jazz as a part of that life and as one of our most significant cultural expressions.

Remembering Song is not a complete history of New Orleans

traditional jazz. Such a work would have to be far grander
in scope than this one, and I have chosen the word "encounters" in the secondary title to indicate another sort of intention. What I have tried for here is to position readers to see
and to feel the *living circumstances* within which jazz was created as I have come to understand these through my own
encounters with the documents and most especially the people and the city of New Orleans itself. I have tried to take
readers inside the history of New Orleans jazz while at the
same time showing them the relations between that history
and our common life. Such an intention seems to me to indicate an emphasis on life histories securely merged with their
cultural and historical backgrounds instead of sociological or
musicological analysis arranged chronologically. Plainly, one
cannot wholly dispense with these latter, nor with chronology, but in these pages they are subordinated to the former
concerns.

The book does in fact respect chronology to the extent
that its arrangement describes a life cycle. The cycle moves
from the origins of a new music to the deaths of the last
carriers of a folk tradition, a tradition that reaches back to
the beginnings of the Afro-American experience, beyond
to the islands of the Caribbean—and ultimately, to Africa.
In following the curve of this cycle I have chosen to empha-
size certain figures—Buddy Bolden, Bunk Johnson, Freddie
Keppard, Jim Robinson—who are perhaps less well known
than some other figures—Jelly Roll Morton, King Oliver, and
Louis Armstrong. This emphasis is not whim, and still less is
it the manifestation of the desire to pose as an adept in the
arcana of jazz history. Rather, Bolden and the others whose
lives and contributions I try to evoke better suit my purpose
of deepening and extending the general understanding of
the cultural and historical significance of this music by drawing attention to its more obscured reaches. There is much
more to the New Orleans story and to the whole history of
jazz than the "star approach" would indicate. The artists I

have chosen to discuss herein are to be seen as symbolic figures as well as actual humans who achieved, erred, suffered,
and died, and I hope that by the time the last pages are
turned, readers will indeed appreciate the symbolic qualities
as well as feel the human dimensions. So, those who expect
that a book on New Orleans jazz would naturally feature its
first—and perhaps greatest—synthesizing genius (Morton), its
first nationally prominent exponent (Oliver), and its greatest
virtuoso (Armstrong), are here requested to hold in suspen-
sion for a while their disappointments and irritations. Morton, Oliver, and Armstrong do in fact appear here and there
in these pages, but the scope is broader and they are merged
within it.

As if such disclaimers were not sufficient, I have used several terms throughout that call for further comment. The
first is "colored." In the 1960s many came to feel angry or
embarrassed by the use of this word; it has generally been
avoided since. I have used it here because it is serviceable.
In writing about the racial mixtures that have historically
characterized the nonwhite population of New Orleans,
plainly I could not use "black" as an all-embracing term.
Where some nonwhites referred to themselves as "Creoles,"
others as "Negroes," and where still other mixtures were de-
noted by the terms "octoroon" and "quadroon," the writer
must simply brave current fashion, however legitimate he may
feel it to be. I have used "colored," then, where I have occasion to refer in general to New Orleans nonwhites. I have
used "Creole" to refer to mixed bloods who knew themselves
by that name. I have used "black" to refer to those nonwhites whose racial mixture is less obvious where it exists
at all.

A second word is "jazz," and its etymology has its own story
to tell of racial barriers. The word is not native to the musical tradition discussed herein and seems not to have been
used until the second decade of this century. When it did
come into use it was commonly spelled "jass," and its ante-

cedent was a vulgar term for either sexual intercourse or seminal fluid. That it should have been attached to the new music is an index both of the low esteem in which the white world held the new music and of the environment to which the music was so often relegated.

Under either spelling, jazz became a way of playing any kind of music, whether Sousa marches, French quadrilles, country blues, or classic Joplin ragtime. As it developed in New Orleans, it was marked by a pronounced rhythmic bias, a preference for inflected notes, and a tendency to lift lines of melodic embellishment and improvisation away from a strict adherence to the rhythmic beat. New Orleans jazz, as Jelly Roll Morton observed, was at its best a style supple enough to accommodate any music from operatic airs to barrelhouse blues. Throughout its history, its greatest practitioners—Morton himself, Duke Ellington, Art Tatum—have demonstrated that jazz, whether traditional, swing, or modern, has retained its remarkable suppleness, its capacity to absorb other musics while remaining true to itself.

However supple and various, jazz has not yet fully escaped its twilight zone of bars, drugs, and prostitution.* Many of its current artists are understandably bitter about this persistent condition, and they avoid using the word "jazz" for this reason. I sympathize with their preference for substitutes such as "black classical music," or "Afro-American music," or simply "the music." But in the absence of a truly compelling and descriptive alternative, I have used "jazz." I do so with some reluctance and ask readers to remain aware throughout of what lies embedded in this familiar word.

---

*Despite its gradual rise toward respectability, more than a whisper of the old opprobrium still clings to this music. In recent years a news and finance magazine sought to impress potential subscribers with the seriousness of its content by advertising that it was "not jazzy." And when we say, "Don't hand me that jazz," we mean, "Don't try to fool me with misleading noise; talk straight." Similarly, if something is said to be "jazzed up," we understand that it is flashy—and perhaps more show than substance.

Two other terms used here are often conflated with jazz but should be distinguished from it. These are "ragtime" and "blues." The early jazz musicians, no respecters of distinctions that were for the most part unimportant to them, often used "ragtime" interchangeably with "jazz" and left the relationship between blues and jazz unstated.

Blues should be used to denote a musical tradition that like jazz has its roots deep in the Afro-American experience. Its major components would appear to be the African-derived worksong, the field holler, and Anglo-Scots balladry and hymns. But the heart of the blues is its "blue notes," those wailing, seemingly off-pitch notes that scholars have traced back to West African vocal and instrumental styles. Often these blue notes have been mistaken for minor harmonies in the European harmonic system. Actually, as James Lincoln Collier has pointed out in his deft analysis of them, "they are neither major . . . nor minor . . . but lie somewhere in between." In playing or singing the blues, he writes, the blue notes "replace the third and seventh in the ordinary diatonic scale: E and B in the C scale."

The blues as a distinct form probably does not go back much before 1890. But Afro-American singers and musicians had been doing what we might call primitive blues for decades before this. During and after Reconstruction, itinerant musicians had increasing contact with each other, and this served to stabilize the form. They also began drifting into the urban areas of the South (and gradually the North), bringing with them the sound of the country blues. In New Orleans the resident musicians heard this country music and learned to play it. In the development of the New Orleans style and canon, blues became vital, as we shall see. But while jazz musicians then and subsequently found blues a rich fund of inspiration, blues is not jazz, and it has its own separate history. Robert Palmer, in *Deep Blues*, has written the most recent and thorough account of that story, taking it from the Mississippi Delta through rhythm and blues, to rock and roll.

For another and wonderfully suggestive look at the blues, I recommend Paul Oliver's *Conversations with the Blues.*

As for "ragtime," its history resembles that of blues insofar as its component parts were present in the South and the Midwest long before it became a recognized form. Here the ultimate derivation would appear to be the syncopated banjo and fiddle playing of plantation Afro-Americans. In their playing normally weak beats were given the same value as strong or accented ones, and the resulting music possessed a propulsive, forward drive that was intimately associated with dance. Other significant ancestral influences were "coon songs," "cakewalks," and marching-band music. Coon songs and cakewalks were adaptations of Afro-American dance music and song made by white minstrel troupers from the 1830s to the 1890s. Thomas D. Rice (1806–1860), for example, the "father of American minstrelsy," got the material for his famous song "Jim Crow" from a crippled slave hostler. He also got powerful inspiration from the songs of a black New Orleans street vendor named "Cornmeal." After the Civil War, the music of the marching bands was tremendously popular and remained so into the first years of the twentieth century. The characteristic 4/4 rhythm of the march may still be heard thundering in the left hand of classic ragtime compositions.

Ragtime as it emerged in the midst of the 1890s was based on suitelike combinations of the old syncopated dance music, on coon songs and cakewalks, and on marching-band music. Its first great exponent, as we now know, was Scott Joplin, who always stressed that ragtime was strictly written music, that it was not a vehicle for improvisation or "vamping," as he put it, nor was it to be speeded up. Of course, this is exactly what happened to his rags and those of the other ragtime composers once they had been heard by the New Orleans musicians at the turn of the century. Many of the compositions of Joplin, Tom Turpin, Louis Chauvin, James Scott, and Joseph Lamb are extremely demanding to perform, and it may be that in some instances the early players' inability to faithfully execute them resulted in the "ragging up" of rags: i.e., tearing up the score and improvising from it. Technical deficiencies, however, are hardly an adequate explanation of the players' general preference for reworking any music that came their way. In any case it is certain that by about 1905, ragtime pieces were central to the repertoires of the New Orleans bands and that the players took characteristic liberties with them. The full story of ragtime is to be found in Rudi Blesh and Harriet Janis's *They All Played Ragtime*, and, somewhat more technically, in William Schaefer's and Johannes Reidel's *The Art of Ragtime*.

To be sure, these are rough distinctions I have made here, and they will make those people squirm who have devoted entire monographs to these subjects. Still, for the audience I have in mind they should serve well enough. For readers wishing further and more precise information, I have suggested source works both here and in the Notes.

F.T.
Santa Fe, New Mexico

Contents

REMEMBERING SONG

(*Left*) Jim Robinson on St. Philip Street (Author photo)
(*Right*) Magnolia Plantation (Author photo)

Bill Russell (Author photo)

(*Above*) E. W. Kemble's drawing of a dance at Congo Square, done to illustrate George Washington Cable's articles on New Orleans black life in the February and April (1886) issues of *Century Magazine*. The spire of St. Louis Cathedral can be seen in the distance.
(*Right*) Only known photograph of Buddy Bolden, standing second from left. The date is variously given, but it is probably about 1905. The other players are Jimmy Johnson, bass, Willie Cornish, valve trombone, William Warner, clarinet, Brock Mumford, guitar, and Frank Lewis, clarinet. (Courtesy of Donald M. Marquis)

Willie Humphrey (Author photo)

(*Above left*) Bunk Johnson (Courtesy of the Al Rose Collection in the Hogan Jazz Archives, Tulane University) (*Below*) Louis Keppard (Author photo)

I. The Story Behind a Sound

Sound is probably the most pervasive phenomenon in our daily lives. We live amidst an aural universe, a symphony of sounds punctuating our days—clicks, creaks, roars, songs, the beating of our own blood—and anyone who has suffered temporary deafness will never forget the shocking surprise of life in a soundless world, how everything from balance to our view of the behavior of others is profoundly affected.

Precisely because sound is so pervasive it is much taken for granted in life as well as in letters, and it is rarely given important place in our reconstructions of the past. Proust, who spent so much time in recollection, did so in the silence of cork-lined apartments and regarded smell as the most historically evocative of the senses. Written history, which we might suppose would be filled with sound, is often curiously silent on the page except for reports of the sounds of words.

This is a book about a sound and especially about the history lying behind that sound. The sound is that of the astonishing folk music created in New Orleans late in the last century and now called "jazz." The history of that sound is complex and densely textured; it is also popularly misunderstood and but partially documented. For a long time the music was neglected by historians so that portions of it have vanished forever, leaving gaps which we fill with speculation, rumor, and private hunches. But this book shows how much of the history of this sound still remains, how much has survived our neglect and misunderstanding.

Any of us could have had the encounters with the New Orleans musical tradition described in these pages, at least potentially. When he wrote that the knowledge of history is "sheerly potential," the Dutch historian Huizinga was, I think, referring to the truth that all of us could investigate aspects of the past, but only a few of us can actually allow ourselves to do so. In the matter of New Orleans jazz this is precisely the case. The city itself is slightly off the New York/Los Angeles cultural axis, but it is surely there on our mental maps, and many of us have visited it. While there we have either sought out or been exposed to some vestige of its most distinctive music. But there are not many who would think to trouble themselves by exploring the content, so to speak, of that sound we know so well, that seems to us the very essence of all jazz. Such an exploration we leave to the writers, if indeed the possibility of it occurs to us at all.

As far as jazz in general and New Orleans jazz in particular are concerned, we have not been as well served as might be. Not many books on jazz have offered invitations to the nonspecialist with a general interest in American history. There are a very few first-rate works on jazz, and there are a number of indispensable books on New Orleans jazz and jazz history without which this work could not have been written. Still, when we ponder the bibliography of jazz we can hardly fail to be struck by the fact that more than eighty years after its creation, the music still awaits its first major writer, its first major historical evaluation. To my knowledge, there has never even been a moderate best-seller on the music. When we think of all the less worthy subjects that have received extensive treatments and warm receptions over this period, we ought to be astonished. And when we reflect further on the fact that some of our first-rate literary talents have chosen to expend their energies chronicling the lives and deaths of murderers and movie queens, we have to wonder whether there is something in the music itself that is intimidating.

From the music's very beginnings in the 1890s the players themselves have been trying to speak to us, to tell us what their music means to them and to us. Mostly we have heard only what we wished and have filtered out what was disturbing, which is, of course, what we try to do with the sounds of our everyday lives. At the turn of the century, those around New Orleans who had been exposed to the new sound and knew where it was coming from thought of it as slave music played by "coons" whose improvisations were the mistakes of the unaccomplished. A few years later when jazz first attracted national attention, it did so as novelty noise. Still later Americans danced to somewhat sanitized, though often very attractive, jazz arrangements. Then the music changed again and was no longer dance music at all. Many were puzzled by this last development, then offended, and at last bored.

It is as if we too, like our unhelpful writers, have been intimidated by something in the music. It is as if we hear an interior sound in jazz that prevents us from embracing it in the ways we so obviously have its derivatives, pop music and rock. Jazz, we obscurely sense, is hard to take at the level of mere entertainment, because however little we may know of it, of the history that went into its sound, we know enough to feel that it cuts too deeply into some unresolved national dilemmas to be casually accepted or lived with comfortably on a daily basis. We hear in that interior sound an intensity of purpose and aspiration that fends off an easy familiarity. In the early days in New Orleans the players called that interior sound "hot," and this is still a useful word for its connotative values. Rock is the huge noise of cynicism and despair. The lovely melodies and clever lyrics of our best songwriters can brighten our lives like a glass of champagne. But jazz is the sound of life being lived at the limits, dangerous as an element that can burn.

This interior sound, this hotness at the heart of all jazz, is a direct bequest to the music from its New Orleans beginnings. More specifically it is the legacy of the conditions of Afro-American life in that place during the last half of the nineteenth century. In order to understand something of the interior sound that the early New Orleans players put into the music for all time, we must explore that world in which—and to some measure in spite of which—they created something so new, so radically different, that after all the intervening years, the conventionalizations, popularizations, the trivializing of the authentic tradition, their music still has the power to surprise, even to unsettle us. Such an exploration is the matter of these chapters.

No historical explanation can hope finally to account for art, and still less this art, since between the urge to create out of life's given conditions and the acts of creation themselves there lie the fathomless depths of the spirit. It is from these depths that the unknown notes must flow, tumbling over each other, in triumph and toward it. But history can tell us somthing of the conditions within which creativity has occurred, and an understanding of these can help us to an appreciation of that creativity. Such is my intention and my hope.

II

My own route to an appreciation of the story behind the New Orleans sound was predictable only in its circuitousness. It is probably impossible now to grow up anywhere in

America without coming to some awareness of New Orleans jazz, if only to recognize its distinctive ensemble voicing and the face of its greatest ambassador, Louis Armstrong. But growing up in Chicago as I did, there might have been a slight edge, for we knew that our city had been the place to which many of the early New Orleans stars had migrated in this century's second decade, that in fact Chicago had replaced New Orleans as the jazz capital of the world. If we didn't know anything specific about the clubs on State Street or the Austin High group that had so closely followed the recorded work of the Original Dixieland Jazz Band and the New Orleans Rhythm Kings in the early 1920s, we knew in a generalized way *about* them. It was clear, too, that Chicago in the 1950s still regarded itself as a jazz town, a "toddlin' town," more than thirty years after the first New Orleans bands had brought their music to the cafés and cabarets of the South Side. Georg Brunis, the veteran New Orleans trombonist, we heard regularly at the 1111 CLUB, though in those days his performances featured as much comedy as playing. Brunis was also occasionally at Jazz Limited as was Chicago's most famous gift to the music, Muggsy Spanier. We frequented both spots; in the egalitarian Chicagoland tradition club owners asked no questions about anyone's age.

There was more of the New Orleans presence available to Chicago kids if they knew where to listen. On Sunday nights from ten to eleven the powerful beam of station WWL, New Orleans, cut through the country sounds of the South, various radio theaters, and sobering end-of-the-week news analyses to bring us live jazz "from atop the Roosevelt Hotel in beautiful downtown New Orleans." In our darkened bedroom, the lighted dial of the set between our beds, my brother and I attended every note, every crowd whistle and stomp, as Tony Almerico and his All-Stars, featuring Lizzie Miles and Buglin' Sam Dekemel, came right at us through the distances of night and geography. It was only after some years that I ever saw these names in print and then began to think of the persons they represented, the lives behind the sounds.

Meanwhile, my musical taste evolved in a way that reproduced in microcosm larger patterns. That is to say, I moved from my allegiance to New Orleans jazz on into swing, captivated there for a few years by Benny Goodman and Count Basie and the early Lester Young—smooth, vibrato-less, the new voice—and then at last on into modern jazz. From this latter vantage point I found myself regarding "dixieland" as tame, predictable, even primitive.* Once, during this advanced stage of ignorance, I had the remarkable opportunity to meet Louis Armstrong and have dinner with him, a reward for having sold the most tickets to his Winnetka concert. It was a nice dinner and all that, and I recall the opulence of the suburban home where the dinner was held, but I must confess that I then privately regarded Armstrong as old-hat, whereas I would have been utterly thrilled to have met, say, the modern trumpeters Maynard Ferguson or Stu Williamson. It was as if station WWL had grown faint of signal so that in the minutes before sleep we no longer heard Almerico's All-Stars but instead recordings of George Shearing, Dave Brubeck, and the newer West Coast players.

Thus New Orleans music dropped slowly, attended by a lingering regret amounting almost to a guilt, down through the layers of memory and value, existing finally like the argot and nicknames of childhood: things to which you were emotionally attached yet felt you had lived far enough beyond to be embarrassed by. And this without my having even

---

*"Dixieland" is another vexing term. It came into popular usage in the 1940s, when it was used to refer to music patterned on the traditional New Orleans style, whether loosely derived from it (as in the case of white bands like the Original Dixieland Jazz Band or the New Orleans Rhythm Kings) or in a more direct line of descent (as in the case of Louis Armstrong's bands or the then current revival groups led by Bunk Johnson, Sidney Bechet, and others).

sensed anything of the cultural and historical significance of what I had once so greatly loved.

III

So it might have remained had not the Byzantine vagaries of research brought me into a new and more intense encounter with New Orleans, its traditions and history. At the end of March 1963, I found myself trainbound south out of Philadelphia for New Orleans to conduct fieldwork there on a local legend that had flourished briefly at the end of the last century. The legend was that of a gambler and killer named Aaron Harris. Harris himself had little to do with jazz, but he had been one of those who made up the audiences of the earliest years, and he had known Jelly Roll Morton and Bunk Johnson. In Alan Lomax's *Mister Jelly Roll* I found several references to Harris, including a blues Morton had composed about him. Lomax had done his New Orleans fieldwork in the 1940s, but the world he had patiently reconstructed was the city's underworld as it had existed in the years 1885–1917. That was also the world I sought, and *Mister Jelly Roll* was my only guide to it.

I discovered as soon as I cleared the depot that my guidebook was no longer very serviceable. The old District that had been the locus of the underworld no longer existed. Basin Street, Rampart, Bienville, Bourbon—they were all still there, but their courses had been so diverted by civic centers, hospitals, and housing projects that their signposts were more misleading than informative. New Orleans seemed another city altogether, one that bore no resemblance to that older one I sought nor acknowledged any relationship to it.

Still, as I walked the sunstruck banquettes, passed beneath the sharp-shadowed arcades, spent afternoons in the bars and oyster houses, hunting out those who might know something of that old legend and its apparently vanished world—the world of Jelly Roll and the old port city, bustling and glinting here, a downriver magnet for all of the great valley that lay above it—I began to get the curious, exciting feeling that here at least the past was not passed, only neglected, or in hiding, or buried, but yet *here*, recoverable.

Partly this growing feeling came to me out of the architecture, partly out of the natural environment. Not only in the French Quarter, the Vieux Carré, but also in the adjacent sections, once called Uptown and Downtown; the shapes of the old buildings and their details spoke in muffled accents of a past they held onto somewhere within their shuttered recesses. Overtopped, squeezed by convention centers, hotels, parking garages, and municipal structures, these native wood survivors were still here, presenting narrow and suggestive façades for those with the will to ponder.

Then, there is the heaviness of the city's environment: you can feel it tug at you as you walk the streets or sit in the parks, and when you visit St. Louis Cemetery No. 1 (the city's oldest), you can *see* it, for here the tombs are precariously raised above the sucking, water-sluiced ooze that underlies all. It is the big river that owns the whole delta and that is forever attempting to reclaim whatever bits of it have been raised above their natural level. The first act of civilizing on this site was in 1718 when Governor Bienville's convict corps of engineers began dredging, diking, and filling against the river, amidst the cypress shadows, mosquitoes, and malaria. A less than sanguine observer of French colonial enterprise then observed that these efforts were folly, since the place Bienville had chosen was good for little more than the cultivation of rice, "for river water filters through the soil, and cray fish abound."

In this wet, sucking place it is easy enough to imagine that everything that ever was here still is—that it is all down there someplace in dark, pressed layers, that New Orleans is a giant, slowly settling palimpsest.

IV

How much this was true began to surface for me one afternoon deep in the old Uptown section at the home of Oscar "Chicken" Henry. I had met Henry the afternoon before when he had played with the Eureka Brass Band at a funeral. We had a casual conversation there in the hot street, the old man fooling with his trombone, his parade cap and starched shirt startling in the powerhouse spring sun, and when we discovered that we shared the same birthday (only forty-nine years apart) there was brief laughter and an invitation to visit him at his home.

"You know," he was saying now in his crowded living room, "if we cry on our birthday, it rains forty days.

"I think," he said then, "I must've cried on many a birthday, 'cause I remember on one of 'em my mama wanted to leave me awhile, to go downtown, y'know. And my grandmama, she didn't want to keep me. There was a hornets nest or something up in the corner of the room. Said, 'Laws, I'd rather them bees come down and light on me than to keep that boy till you get back!' "

In and out and around such anecdotes that afternoon Oscar Henry wove the story of his musical life like the melody in a New Orleans band performance. He had put his hands to many other things than his instrument, had been a plasterer and bricklayer, and his feet had stepped to more menial measures than marches and in places other than New Orleans. But always there had been this: the music and its original place.

"How I happened to come back here," he said, "was I got a letter from my Daddy, said he needed some help on a contracting job, y'know. Well, I was in Chicago reading this letter in a hotel room—had a whole fifth of I.W. Harper on the table. And I said, 'Well, I ain't never done nothing for the old man.' So I come back here," dropping his hands flat to his knees, "been here ever since."

Being "here" meant work as a semiskilled laborer with music on the side, an occupational combination I didn't then recognize as standard for men like himself. Then, talking about his jobs, he casually mentioned that originally he'd been a piano player but that his hand had been so badly damaged in an accident that he had switched to the trombone. More than the details of the accident, I recall the evenness of its telling. This, the voice was telling me, this is how life is: nothing special about getting hurt on the job, about working days and playing nights and weekends. In Henry's world these were matters beneath special notice. There were many he had known who had had it tougher, who had not been lucky enough to make it through to union wages and old age. He had his house, scale wages, family. He smiled gently; it had all worked out all right.

"But y'know, it's sad. Everything here is kind of coming to a close. This city," gesturing to the street to be seen through the open door—cars rattling by, kids skating, milk bottles clanking on wooden stoop steps—"they're tearing things down here that can never be replaced. 'Cause there ain't anybody that can do the work anymore that's already here. It's sad. Lizzie Miles, she says she wants to die before they change it all over."

In the shadows of a New Orleans March afternoon you are reminded that it is after all still spring, for there is a sudden chill on the air, a deeper blue to those shadows. Henry had gotten up to shut the door, an old man's response to the drawing up of veins, the fainter beat of blood. Then I told him as he stood by the window looking into the street that my white cabbie had been sure that I'd made a mistake in the address when he saw the neighborhood. Henry laughed. "Now you got to go back the other way, and you won't get a ride out."

He was right. A couple of blocks up there was a line of

cabs at the curb, all their drivers black, and none would take me back to the Quarter. "It ain't discrimination," one told me, elbow over the door, newspaper propped against the steering wheel. "It's just the way things work."

Walking the weary blocks, my "portable" tape recorder pulling at my shoulder sockets, I finally raised St. Louis Cathedral in the heart of the Vieux Carré, the clock spire now etched deep purple against the whitening blue of the sky. Beneath the cathedral lay the moldered ashes of the city's first church and within it the parish records, mutilated by some who sought to obscure forever the shame of the mixed blood of their ancestry. Behind it there was a small enclosed park wherein Creole duelists once drew swords and foolish blood. And farther out behind that, in shadows longer than those thrown by diurnal rhythms, there was Congo Square, slave ground, where feet and drums had improvised a history that now in this place and light I was just beginning to realize.

II. A History of "Hot"

Today if you asked a New Orleans resident the way to Congo Square, you would be likely to draw a blank look. Or, if the resident were so inclined, you might encounter the hostility meted out to traveling racial troublemakers, for the name "Congo" is still a bell-ringer. Even if you asked the way to Beauregard Square, you might not get any help, for these days about the only distinguishing feature of the place in question is its proximity to the Municipal Auditorium.

When you get there you can see why this is so, for there isn't much to see: just a small park at the nether end of the Vieux Carré, a few benches under the big oaks, fountain, walks, grass, and behind it, dwarfing it, the big and undistinguished auditorium. Rampart Street, which you must cross to get to the park, is four lanes now, and, because it is one of the few thoroughfares around the Quarter where you can make some time, the traffic hurtles along it at an alarming rate. Most people you see sitting in the park seem to be taking breathers from the adventure of crossing Rampart.

The noise of the traffic and the presence of the auditorium make it hard to visualize what the place would have been like a century and a half ago. The trees and the bit of grass are not very suggestive clues. But now, turn around and look back at the way you have come, and something may occur to you. Look down Orleans Street past the site of the Orleans Ballroom, where in the last century they held the Quadroon Balls at which the white gentry bid on likely Quadroon women. Just past there you can see where Royal Street runs by the shrubbery of St. Anthony Square, and behind that rises the spire of St. Louis Cathedral. It is not a long distance—only four pleasant blocks—but a century and a half ago the distance separated two worlds. At one end was the Place d'Armes, the hub of the white man's world, and, as the New Orleans writer George Washington Cable aptly expressed it, "In the early days it stood for all that was best. . . ." The "Place Congo," as it was then known, was at the other end of the street, outside the city walls, and "at the opposite end of everything." The white man's plaza, Cable observed, "had the army and navy on its right and left, the court-house, the council-hall and the church at its back, and the world before it. The black man's was outside the rear gate, the poisonous wilderness on three sides and the proud man's contumely on its front." *This* is a perspective that can help us to visualize something of Congo Square and its meanings.

When Cable wrote of Congo Square in 1886 it had become Beauregard Square in honor of the Confederate general. But among most of the city's nonwhite populace the square probably still went by its old name, and they would have had memories of the dances performed there as recently as the year before.

The most recent dancers at Congo Square had been, of course, freed people, General Beauregard's efforts notwithstanding. But further back into the century they had been slaves. Sunday in slavery times was the one day in the week these people could look forward to. The New Orleans whites danced every day of the week including Sunday, for dancing, like music, was a local passion. Perhaps it was for this reason that they allowed their slaves their own Sunday dances.

Reports of dances held at various locations take us back into the eighteenth century. Slaves danced on the levee, at a campground on Lake Pontchartrain, and at a place that must be Congo Square: an 1819 letter from New Orleans remarked that on Sundays the "African slaves meet on the green, by the swamp, and rock the city with their Congo dances." As Sidney Bechet, the great New Orleans reed player, imagined these Sundays, the slave would awaken "and start to be a slave and then maybe someone would tell him: 'Hell no. Today's Sunday, man. . . . Today's free day.' And then he'd hear the drums from the square. First one drum, then another one answering it. Then a lot of drums. Then a voice, one voice. And then a refrain, a lot of voices joining in and coming into each other."

Bechet was born in 1897, more than a decade after the dances had ceased, so his memory of them is improvised out of what he had heard and what he knew had to be true. "Hot" player that he was, he knew that the sound he breathed from the bell of his horn had come out of these dances and all that had gone into them—the long history of the African past and that darker tale of his people taken out of Africa, to the islands, to this place, to the one piece of ground that— on Sundays—they fully possessed.

We also have eyewitnesses. On these Sunday afternoons, after mass, after the visitings and the dinner, a crowd of whites would gather outside the low fence and turnstile that marked off the square to watch the black folks dance and sing in native ways. Some, including the prominent northern architect Benjamin Latrobe and George Washington Cable, took notes. Latrobe's notes from 1819 are especially valuable for the clear view they give of the survival of African music and musical customs. His sketches of the instruments—drums of various sizes, rattles and auxiliary percussive instruments, and the African progenitor of the banjo—leave no doubt that the slaves had persisted in fashioning their instruments on the models of their lost homeland. The language of the singers and the patterns of the dances, Latrobe guessed, were also African, for in his wide travels he had never encountered their like. "The allowed amusements of Sunday," he wrote, "have . . . perpetuated here those of Africa. . . ." And in a manner typical of the time, he concluded that he had "never seen anything more brutally savage, and at the same time dull & stupid, than this whole exhibition."

In one respect at least Latrobe was right: the Congo Square gatherings were very much in the West African mode. The music was intensely communal in nature, there being no distinction between performers and audience—all were performers. The music's antiphonal structure—its call-and-response pattern—emphasized this communal quality, as did the integral relationship between music, song, and dance. The pronounced rhythmic bias and the preference for instruments that would produce a clashing, clattering, clangorous accompaniment to the rhythm of the drums—these, too, are characteristic of that region from which the majority of the New World's slaves were drawn.

The sounds made by the hundreds of participants there in the matted, dusty clearing must have been enormous. Welling from the drums of hollowed logs, the wooden horns, calabashes, animal jawbones scraped with keys, and vials of buckshot attached to wrists and ankles produced thunderous waves of native music that washed over the black crowd and buffeted the white audience. Above all there was the sound of the human voice, sonorous, wailing, improvisatory, telling of a history the whites could not know. And all the while at the opposite end of Orleans Street was the cathedral, the placid promenade, the tended gardens of another world.

Some of the dancers had been brought here directly from Africa, others by way of the West Indies. It was on the islands that the slaves, struggling to make sense of their tattered lives, had over time created a powerful syncretic religion. To these people the complete severing of tribal and family ties rendered existence meaningless; only by somehow remaining in contact with the past, with the spirits of the ancestors, could they make sense of life. The strikingly similar religions of two West African tribes, the Dahomeans and the Yorubas (enemies though they had been), showed all the captives how these ties might be maintained, though the people were now separated by all those gray, watery miles from the old places of worship and the bones of the great dead. These religions were based on a veneration of that vanished place and the ancestors, but they were not dependent on material items nor on actual touch with the place itself. Instead they utilized memory and memory-invoking rituals to maintain these vital associations, both of which could survive the physical rupture of deportation. On Trinidad, Martinique, Cuba, Jamaica, and especially Haiti, the Dahomeans and the Yorubas took the lead in the creation of new rituals based partly on old ones and partly on present circumstances. In dances to percussive music and in the trancelike states thus induced, the slaves could be transported out of present circumstances back into the bosom of the African past, to Guineé, place of origin, imagined in the new religion, voodoo, as an island beneath the sea where the gods have permanent residence. There is good reason to believe that this is in fact what was going on in the dances at Congo Square and that the dance ground itself may have been conceived as one of those special crossroads where the plane of the secular world is intersected by the vertical thrust of the spirit world: a place of access.

The white masters who countenanced the dances that rocked the city's Sundays took essentially the same view of them as had the master class on the islands. That view was the long Latin-Catholic one, developed through the church's centuries of missionizing and converting among the heathen of the globe: in the fullness of Christian time, they thought, such native survivals as these would atrophy and then die out. It was not essential therefore to expend valuable energies in suppressing behavior that was ultimately doomed and that was essentially harmless, even entertaining in a primitive way. For this reason the New Orleans slaves were allowed their "entertainments" well over a century after slaves elsewhere on the North American mainland had been denied them.

Something else persisted here, too, long after it had been suppressed everywhere else: the international slave trade. The Lafitte brothers had established the lucrative practice of smuggling slaves up Barataria Bay to within sight of the city's spires. Well after the trade was interdicted in 1808 and after the Lafittes had been run out of the business others took it up and continued in it until the eve of the Civil War. Most of those who entered New Orleans through this clandestine route were straight out of Africa, which means that here as nowhere else in North America the African influence continued strong well into the nineteenth century. Alice Zeno, mother of the twentieth-century jazz clarinetist George Lewis, remembered walking the city's streets with her grandmother and pausing before a site as the old woman pointed at it, remembering: that is where they sold niggers.

All of this should help us to understand what was on Sidney Bechet's mind when he called his music a "memory thing": it was the memory of Africa, of the sundered past, and of that deathless drive to recover that past and so be whole once more, if only for a little while, if only for a day. "It was primitive and it was crude," Bechet said of the music of Congo Square, "but down at the bottom of it—inside it, where it starts and gets into itself—down there it had the same thing there is at the bottom of ragtime. It was already born and making in the music they played at Congo Square."*

At nine o'clock in slavery times the music and dancing at the square were ended with a premonitory cannon shot fired above the sounds of the instruments, the drumming feet, the calling voices. Here was that imperative sound from the world at the other end of Orleans Street, telling the dancers that it was time to go "home," time to cease remembering, time to be a slave again. So the "entertainers" left their improvised stage, and the whites, benign in tolerance, turned again to their own affairs.

Yet even after the official end of slavery, after the Emancipation Proclamation they celebrated at the old square, New Orleans blacks continued intermittently to hold festivities there, for there continued to be the need for such expressions of communality. Though they were legally now merged with the rest of the city's population, there was in fact much that segregated them from both the whites and the colored Creoles. Through the sullen years of Reconstruction when New Orleans was a federal garrison and into the period of white backlash during which the new freedoms were steadily abridged or nullified through the withdrawal of federal protections, the institution of Jim Crow laws, and race riots, New Orleans blacks struggled along with a staggering set of handicaps: poor health, gross poverty, illiteracy, lack of trade skills, and the social instability that was the legacy of generations of enslavement. These they brought to the task of competing in a locally shrinking labor market set within national con-

---

*Bechet uses the term "ragtime," as many of the early players did, to refer to what we would now call "jazz." It does not refer here specifically to the written ragtime compositions of Joplin et al, though as I have indicated in the Preface, these compositions in various forms were staples of jazz bands from around 1900 to 1918. Bechet's "ragtime" (jazz) rather refers to a style in which *any* music could be played, whether ragtime, blues, or Tin Pan Alley songs.

ditions of economic uncertainty. The occasional gatherings at Congo Square were part of an effort to lighten this burden by retaining something of the old communal feeling amidst the new conditions that often seemed as frightening and bewildering as they did hopeful.

There were other efforts at lightening the load. Blacks could now form social clubs and benevolent associations where they might come together for social comfort and a few meager economic protections, such as the guarantee of a decent burial. They could go to cabarets and dance halls in the nights after their days of work—or of looking for work. They could spend precious dollars on newly available luxury items such as dress clothes and spirits. In vain did the town's black leaders and black newspapers inveigh against these latter costly diversions, for life had been too hard under slavery and that under freedom too grudging for many to deny themselves such pleasures as were available.

The counsel of thrift and deferred gratification was further undermined by the failure of the Freedman's Savings and Trust in 1874. Here at a stroke vanished the pitiful savings of thousands of people, and many of them would never again trust in a future. Perhaps it was best after all to live for the moment. Who could tell what tomorrow might bring? Would there even be a tomorrow? For too many there would not: John Blassingame gives a frightening black infant mortality rate of four hundred and fifty per thousand in the New Orleans of 1880 and a life expectancy of a paltry thirty-six years, a full decade less than the average for local whites.

So, after the days in the cotton pickeries, bent in shapeless garments over their tasks; after the last barrels had been hauled and stacked on the long wharves; after the shoeshine box had been put away, the dray horses stabled, the barbershop shut down, and the last wisps of black hair swept out, then there might still be something in the night before another day and its menial duties.

The cabarets, perhaps. Narrow places, one room wide and three deep, they reached back from the street-front bar to the middle gambling room, then to the back room of saw-dusted floor, bench-lined walls, and tiny bandstand. This was for the dancers. In the front room the high-powered beer was poured into the sweating lard buckets. In the gambling room life took its chances. In the back room the dark dancers moved together while the band—perhaps mandolin, guitar, string bass, and cornet—played quadrilles, waltzes, mazurkas, polkas, schottisches. In the last years of the century the late night carried the sound of the blues, tough and slow-driving, the Afro-American national anthem, played here until dawn's early light signaled the end of one day and the beginning of another.

The escape into music came readily to New Orleans blacks, mostly because of what has already been suggested, but also because they lived in a music-mad city. Eighteenth- and nineteenth-century travelers to New Orleans were consist-ently astonished by the amount and quality of music that could be heard from street corner seranaders, guitar-strum-ming swains, street vendors who sang their wares, marching bands, and singers and pianists in the parlors of private homes. At a time in the nineteenth century when most American cities had no resident opera company, New Or-leans supported three. There was a constant demand in the city for musicians of all sorts, and this remained true through war, epidemics, occupation, Reconstruction, and backlash.

Men of color had always been used as musicians for pop-ular entertainments, and increasingly so as they acquired what was often designated a "peculiar facility" with European in-struments. To the whites they seemed to approach their in-struments and their music in a unique and curious way. "Did you ever hear Negroes play the piano by ear?" the writer Lafcadio Hearn asked a friend in a letter from New Orleans.

"Sometimes we pay them a bottle of wine to come here and play for us. They use the piano exactly like a banjo." This instrument and the fiddle were presumed to be the natural ones for colored musicians, the first because it was an African instrument, the other because they had long ago taken it up in the country parishes. But now they were finding their ways to a variety of instruments as their opportunities slowly broadened in the years following emancipation.

By far the most favored colored musicians in New Orleans had been the *gens de couleur*, the colored Creoles. Intermediates, the issue of unlawful congress between separated races, these proud people had enjoyed a precarious but real freedom before the war and had created a significant third-stream culture. They monopolized the skilled trades and crafts, owned extensive properties (including slaves), followed professions, and in some cases were able to send their children abroad for education and refinement. A good many were accomplished musicians with academic training: the European musicians so much in demand were not adverse to teaching those nonwhites who could afford lessons. Like the whites—who, for the love of that white blood that flowed in them, had allowed them their freedom—the polite colored Creoles considered music a normal part of the home routine. So when Reconstruction became backlash and the colored Creoles became merely colored, lost their privileged status, and were forced into economic and social competition with the blacks from whom they had previously held themselves stiffly aloof, it was they who commanded the most prestigious and best-paying musical jobs.

For whites it was unthinkable that a gentleman should be a professional musician; that was work for servants. The Creoles had adopted this same value, so it was demeaning for them now to do for pay and strangers what had once been done for manners and family. But jobs were scarce, the days of privilege done. Perhaps then it was not so terrible to play your instrument for pay, the clear, light, correct tones

sounding now at the balls, lawn parties, and municipal cele-
brations of the whites, and especially in the marching-band
music that was the rage in the half-century after the war.

Such a musician could also hire out as a music teacher.
Increasingly their pupils were blacks, who for the first time
might have a few extra dollars for an instrument and lessons, dimly foreseeing perhaps some additional income from
a nighttime and Sunday career as a band musician, cabaret
player, or fish-fry serenader. Increasingly as the century drew
to a close the master musicians found themselves in musical
competition with those who had been their pupils or else
were self-taught.

It was bitter to these masters to discover that the blacks
had something no training could teach, a way of playing un-
heard before. Band music and polite dance music for white
occasions the colored Creoles understood: it was written music, very precise, and some of it quite demanding. But to
play for blacks, to play for their occasions and dances was
another matter. Here something more was required than
training could provide: it was memory. Memory of that past
reached back for at Congo Square (when Latrobe had visited
it he had noted less than a dozen light-skinned faces in a
crowd of more than five hundred). Memory of the long history of loss and deprivation that finally found its form of
expression in the blues somewhere in the century's last two
decades. To play for these people you had to have the sound
of their story, and this was something the Creoles had spent
more than a hundred years denying.

The black players had that sound. Much closer to the West
African tradition of a highly rhythmic, improvisational music, communal in nature and integrally associated with dance,
they transformed every music they attempted, including now
the new ragtime numbers that were tinkling into the city on
the fingers of itinerant piano players out of the Midwest.

The poet Robert Duncan has said that innovation can come
only from what we do not know. That may not be as useful

an explanation of what New Orleans blacks were doing with any music that came to them as is some understanding of their history and cultural heritage; but it does help to explain that feeling of excitement and surprise that the new music produced in its sympathetic listeners. In many instances the black musicians were not readers and did not know the precise direction a number was going to take. They played what they felt, what they knew or sensed of their past.

To whites who chanced to hear this new music it sounded "ragged." But the colored Creoles, competing for some of the same musical jobs, were astonished and baffled. One of them, Alphonse Picou, vividly recalled his first experience trying to play the new way. Born in 1879, when his caste was well embarked on its downhill way to full equality with the blacks, Picou had been given clarinet lessons by his parents; doubtless even in those straitened times they had wished to preserve some of the old amenities. On a day in 1895 when the boy was practicing at home, the neighboring barber overheard him. Like many of his fellows, the barber doubled as a musician, and he quickly obtained the parents' permission to talk to the young Picou. That night Picou found himself at an audition for the weekend band the barber fronted, and he remembered asking the leader where the music was that he was to play. "He said, 'Music? You don't need none.' I said, 'How am I going to play?' He said, 'You're going to come in on the choruses,'" explaining to the bewildered boy that when he could not come in he should just stay out. Picou evidently came in more than he stayed out since that Saturday night he was with the band in a jammed hall on Liberty Street. Auditioning without music was one thing and playing to a crowd without it was another, but the band jumped into the midst of a piece and "the people just clapped their hands. We had to play [each piece] two or three times. . . ." That particular style of "playing without music," he concluded, "was very new to me. I think it was impossible to me! It seemed a sort of style of playing without

notes." Almost sixty years afterward Picou was still playing
the style "without notes," and he has left behind him the
standard clarinet solo in the old New Orleans march "High
Society."

But for every Picou there were many other colored Creoles who found that they could not play the new music, and
even in Picou's playing some heard a whisper of that cool
Creole reserve, as if the interior sound of memory still eluded
him. Sidney Bechet, a Creole whose cultural and musical
identification was with the blacks, took lessons for a short
time from another Creole clarinetist, George Baquet, a contemporary of Picou's. But the correct Creole master had little to teach the pupil who had heard the interior sound of
the music and had intuited the story it told. When his teacher
played the music, Bechet recalled, "there wasn't none of those
growls and buzzes which is a part of ragtime music, which is
the way the musicianer has of replacing different feelings he
finds inside the music and inside himself. . . . There wasn't
none of that in the way he played. I don't know if it was that
Baquet *couldn't* do it, all I know is he *didn't* do it." Leonard
Bechet, brother to the great Sidney, knew what it took and
knew too what he himself lacked. Talking with author and
folklorist Alan Lomax, Leonard put it bluntly: "Now, I'll tell
you . . . a person have to go through all that rough stuff
like Sidney went through to play music like him." Some of
the Creoles, he said, had not gone through that and did not
care to mix with those who had. Picou, for one. "You see,
Picou—Picou's a very good clarinet, but he ain't hot." Then
he got to the bottom of it, to what divided the colored Creoles from the blacks quite as much as that fence and gate
had divided the whites from the dancers at Congo Square:
"You have to play real *hard* when you play for Negroes. You
got to *go* some, if you want to avoid their criticism. You got
to come up to their mark. . . . If you do, you get that drive.
Bolden had it."

II

Not a single participant in the music's formative years fails to invoke the name "Bolden." This is Charles "Buddy" Bolden, who in legend is to this music what Babe Ruth is to baseball, Ford to the automobile. Whether in reminiscences of a black or of a Creole, at some point this man will make a forceful entrance, though his life remains something of a mystery, his sound has vanished, and he exists for us visually in only two images, one a photograph so blotched and scratched that you cannot tell his eyes from the imperfections of age and the original of which has perversely disappeared.

Every genuine folk movement creates its ultimate hero or heroine, and so it is here. Such a figure has a basis in historical fact and functions as a prismatic image through which a total historical experience is concentrated and made readily available to those who have had their parts in it. To the hero are attached attributes and experiences that symbolize those of the group; when they speak of him they are speaking of themselves, for his story is really theirs.

So then, Buddy Bolden: what is there behind his tantalizingly blurred features, inside the cornet he holds so casually against the flat of his palm? Few preliminaries here, for his legend begins in the middle with Bolden already possessed of a heroic inventiveness. Somewhere in the city's Uptown section in the summer of 1895 Bolden stands up before his little band, raised waist-high above the dancers, and improvises a chorus of blues. And then another, and another. The crowd, sensing the advent of the new, roars encouragement, demands that he repeat them. Bolden cannot, for he has already forgotten his latest invention. But he has others, many others. In that night Kid Bolden becomes King Bolden, raised into a strange and singular fame, just as he had raised himself above his band and the crowd in the hot hall.

He can play with unparalleled power all night long, one improvised chorus after another bursting from an instrument he keeps burnished like a woman's leg. But there is something else that is as compelling as his power and inventiveness. It is a history and a style that come from the heart of Uptown, or Niggertown. Black and born the year that Reconstruction ended, it is said that he saw the dances at Congo Square. Later he somehow got hold of a cornet, perhaps a battered little piece left behind in a pawnshop by a departed bandsman of the federal garrison. He teaches himself his own way about it, picking up the sounds native to his neighborhood and class: the street songs, the soul-steeped hymns of the Baptist church across from his house, the blues from corner guitar pickers. He scorns note reading: everything must be by ear and memory; everything must be felt to be played.

He scorns ties and collars, too, wearing his shirt busted open to reveal a workingman's blazing red undershirt stretched across his chest. For like the rest, he is a workingman, spending his daylight hours as a barber. When he leaves First Street in the evenings, passing the now-shuttered barbershop on his way to his real work, a crowd of women follows. One carries his horn, another his watch, a third his coat, and yet another is just hoping.

If he is to play either Lincoln or Johnson Park on the outskirts of town, he pulls the crowds out there by pointing his horn toward the center of town and blowing the blues. He says this is "calling his children home," and they come to his call, running toward those notes that come from them, too. If by chance John Robichaux's band is playing the park opposite, Bolden sees this as a challenge, for Robichaux is a colored Creole, raised by white folks, and his "legitimate" reading band gets the society jobs, playing correctly, serenely, in close-buttoned coats with music stands and charts arranged before them. "Come on, Cornish," Bolden says to his trombonist, "Come on, put your hands through the window." And they put their horns out through the window and blast so high, so seductively that the dancers to Robichaux can hear nothing else and so leave the legitimate bunch to crowd into the presence of the King. "Of course," said the old-time cornetist Bunk Johnson, "the whites said, 'We don't want no King Bolden. Robechaux's [sic] the band.' . . . *They* called Bolden's band a 'routineer' bunch, a bunch of 'fakers.' But amongst the Negroes, Buddy Bolden could close a Robechaux dance up by ten-thirty at night."

Wherever he tours in the outlying parishes the astonished children and their parents drop everything: "It's King Bolden! It's King Bolden's band!" Once, in some country dance hall he blows his horn apart, and one of the local kids becomes an instant celebrity by lending the King his beat-up little cornet. "Buddy laughs like hell. Says, 'Well, pardner, it's better'n nothin'.' " And once, coming through Plaquemine, his playing causes a black boy to exclaim, "I never heard anything like that in my whole life. I'm goin' to New Orleans."

In 1897 town officials rope off a district for prostitution, gambling, and the new music that seems to go with these: the District, the players call it ("Storyville," to us). Here Bolden solidifies his rule, moving nightly through his domain of halls and cabarets: Perseverance Hall, Globe Hall, Come Clean, Big Easy, Few Clothes, Drag Nasty, Funky Butt, Spano's, Tuxedo. . . . At each of these Bolden plays the numbers he has made famous, "Make Me a Pallet on Your Floor," "If You Don't Shake, You Don't Get No Cake," and his theme, "Buddy Bolden's Blues." As in the days of Congo Square which Buddy can see from the bandstand at Globe Hall, this is music for the dancers, and there is an electric sympathy between those on the floor and those on the stand. They tell each other things, and when the King plays "Don't Go Away, Nobody" everyone knows the polite dancing is over and now it will be blues until daybreak.

Sleep? Bolden doesn't need it. He has that staying power, workingman's power. He has a signal to his band, "Don't take down," which means, "Don't put your instruments down. Keep playing." And they keep on, from "can't see 'til can." One morning after another long night Bolden and his band are down on the levee playing for the departure of a shipload of black troops bound for action in the Spanish-American War. When Bolden starts into the blues the troops begin jumping overboard and swimming ashore. His sound is their anthem.

By now it is our century, and the legend of the hero begins to merge into the history of the music he is credited with creating. Whereas previously it existed in a sort of vacuum, unsurrounded by competitors, historyless as it began a history, now it begins to glimmer out from behind the names of the successors to his music. We hear talk of "Storyville," where at any intersection there would be four cabarets, each with its band of younger musicians playing Bolden's music at top volume. Seven-piece bands blared in the big halls of the District or "bucked" each other in musical battles fought from the beds of furniture wagons the bands would hire to advertise the dances. As a band rolled through a neighborhood, a rival group might rumble into view, and then the two would lock wheels to try to play each other down: "Didn't He Ramble" against "Moose March." The winners got the crowd that night, but such was the popularity of the music that there were no real losers—there were always jobs. Thus where before we heard only of King Bolden's band, now we hear of the Columbus Band led by the heavy-lipped power-house cornetist, Tig Chambers; of the Imperial Orchestra headed by Manuel Perez, the best of the Creole cornet players; of the Magnolia Orchestra, organized around 1909 and including in its membership some who would approach legendary status themselves in the course of time. We hear too

of other "kings" of the cornet: Freddie Keppard, Jo
who succeeded him, and Bunk Johnson, who had th
est tone in town. And we learn where the piano playe
in the mirror-spangled parlors of the high-priced
houses where the geniuses Jelly Roll Morton and
Jackson and Sammy Davis earned big tips playing the
improvising dirty songs, and speeding through the de
ing ragtime pieces of Scott Joplin and Tom Turpin
companiment to the naked dances and circus tricks
whores.

In the twenty-two years from the legendary rise of
Bolden to the closing of the District in 1917, the new r
became a recognized style with a standard instrumenta
ensemble sound, and canon of tunes. By 1917 Buddy
den's name was surrounded by others, and he was spoke
in the past tense. For by this time Bolden had ceased to
an active force in the music. It was said that on some date
spring day, playing a long, hot funeral procession, Bud
Bolden "fell out," quit playing, and that he never play
again. "Bolden?" the men said, musing. "Aw, that cat burn
himself out. Always studyin' up something new." "Bolde
Whiskey and women killed him." "Bolden? He blew his brain
out through the horn," said Jelly Roll.

This is the legendary ending for the King, and since it i
legend, it is wholly appropriate. Unlike historiography which
must attempt to sort out probable truths from available evidence, legend deals solely in The Truth as it is felt by those
who celebrate the legend. And The Truth of the legend is
to be found in the sort of hero Bolden was made to be.

This is not a hero of assimilation and upward mobility like
Frederick Douglass and Booker T. Washington. The legendary Bolden accepts the terms of life as he finds it, but he
also attempts to improvise a creative and radically native way
of living with those terms. His music expresses him as he is,
black, Uptown, working class, content to be so as long as his
full humanity is recognized. Thus his legend expresses a

scornful opposition to any behavior that smacks of "pass-ing": Bolden, the collarless, non-reading powerhouse player versus the correct and classically trained Robichaux.

What then of the King's legendary ending? It is a bitter commentary on the perceived circumstances of Afro-American life at the turn of the century as well as a bleak view of the prospects that lay ahead in what some Americans were fondly thinking of as the millennium. For in attempting a creative identification with his circumstances and cultural background, this hero runs headlong into risks and dangers he might have avoided had he but *passively* accepted life's terms. To go mad and to an early grave trying to express yourself and your history, this is a motif expressive of an ag-ony of aspiration as well as a fear of that aspiration and its defeat. Bolden's blue notes, it was said, sounded like his heart was breaking. *That* is the interior sound of this music, the hero's eternal legacy to it. And it is why he can never be forgotten.

Walking the streets of Bolden's old neighborhood you can feel that interior sound of the music, that "hotness," hum-ming up out of places that have changed little since 1895—except to deteriorate. Along First Street things look much the same as they did when Bolden lived here. Now as then this is a predominantly black neighborhood, where in the schoolyard spidery-looking black boys fantasize becoming superstars as they shoot basketballs toward backboards with-out hoops. At the corner of First and Liberty is the barber-shop where Bolden spent some of his daylight hours making arrangements for his band dates. A wooden awning curves around the corner, and there are benches underneath. In-side, on the walls above the two chairs and the mirrors flecked russet with age, are pictures of Lincoln, Booker T. Washing-ton, and Frederick Douglass. Also photos of Jack Johnson and Joe Louis punching and getting punched—that was an-other way to make it out.

Across the street is Bolden's house, 2309, its yellow paint

chipping down to other layers, its high streetward window shuttered. Along here few know that Charles "Buddy" Bolden did not merely disappear from a parade but that he died a hundred miles away in the segregated unit of the state insane asylum where for a quarter century he had rotted away untreated beneath a crude psychiatric label. Probably the historical ending is not as important as the legendary one anyway, for in the latter we see history reliefed, its broad patterns sharply defined for those who will look.

Go up a couple of blocks to Jackson Street where the hulk of the old Longshoreman's Hall stands awaiting the wrecker's ball. In the littered and sunny courtyard that was once a dance hall you can feel that sound. This was a haven built by black workers against the uncertainties and the grim certainties of their America, a place where for a dollar you could dance to music made by your neighbors.

Or go up farther into the old District and enter the narrow coffin that is Perseverance Hall. Mount the handsome staircase that curves in company with the dank, peeling walls until you gain the upper story and its single high-ceilinged room. There amidst the emptiness and the immeasurably gradual pull of the town's wet gravity, think of Bolden and the others. Think of the nameless dancers who moved here to sounds that told them stories. Here in silence and neglect is that sound, history beating against the ear.

III. Bunk's
Back Country Blues

Striving to explain to an historian just what special quality it was that the black players had, Leonard Bechet, Sidney's dentist brother, called it a "drive." It was what Bolden had that the more technically accomplished Manuel Perez didn't. Then Dr. Bechet added, "Bunk had it." Bunk Johnson, he said, "was one of them kind—rough and ready." He was not alone in this opinion, for there were many in the New Orleans musical family who considered Johnson one of Buddy's main boys, a stylistic and maybe even temperamental descendant. Considering the power of the Bolden legend, it is not surprising that Johnson himself did as much as he could to impress this connection in the minds of his listeners.

He had started, Bunk recalled in old age, with Adam Olivier's orchestra, a small outfit led by a cornetist who spent his daylight hours barbering. But then, while still in his identifying uniform of juvenile short pants, Bunk had the thrill of hearing King Bolden at Lincoln Park. "And I got crazy to play with Bolden, and Bolden played my style of music that

I liked. I liked to read . . . but I rather played that head music better—more jazz to it." Bolden, remembered Bunk, had played "mighty much by head" and had made up his own tunes. So he jumped the Olivier band and joined the King: "I was crazy to play blues. Bolden were playing blues of all kinds."

On another occasion Johnson recalled a dialogue between the great, original star and himself, there in the twilight of the park in that summer of '95, Bolden peering down from the bandstand at the teen-ager holding his cornet case with the ribbon his mother always tied around it:

What you got there, boy?

A cornet.

Can you play it?

I can play it.

Can you play the blues, boy?

I can play the blues.

What key do you play the blues in?

Answering now in the flush of confidence, at least as he would much later wish to remember it: Any key you got.

On yet another occasion, this in a letter to jazz historians who had traced him to his western Louisiana obscurity, Johnson staked an even more emphatic claim, telling them that he and King Bolden "were the first men that began playing Jazz in the city . . . and his band had the whole of New Orleans Real Crazy and Running Wild behind it." That, he said, was all you could hear in New Orleans in 1895 and '96, "and they did not have any dixie land Jazz Band in those days."* Now that you have this straight, he concluded, "you are able to go . . . ahead with your book."

By Bunk's own chronology, he was with Bolden, or with

---

*Johnson's disparaging reference here is to the all-white band that aped the styles of the New Orleans colored players even while disdainfully refusing any association with the originators. Calling themselves the Original Dixieland Jazz Band, they were the first to make a big financial success with New Orleans jazz in 1917. See pp. 81–82.

one of the King's several bands, until 1898 when he began the first of the wanderings that were to become a permanent feature of his career. It is thought he went to Texas for a while before returning to become part of the reorganized Bolden main unit when the King fell out forever.

In the new band, Bunk played Bolden's parts, and there is a legendary tale that tells of Buddy forcing his way alone, unattended by the vanished hordes of hangers-on, up to a bandstand on which his youthful successor stood, driving out the slow blues that had been Bolden's signature. Then the crowd fell away to let him pass, and the man, emitting the fallen monarch's negative mana, left the hall behind forever. He returned, legend says, to that First Street barbershop where he sat in shuttered anonymity, playing sacred blues with his Stetson draped over the bell of his cornet, tears of rage and bafflement coursing brokenly down his cheeks.

If Bolden's legend tells us something important about the history of a people through the critical and treacherous post-Reconstruction period, then the life and career of Willie Geary "Bunk" Johnson have something to tell us of that people's subsequent odyssey toward an undifferentiated—and unprotected—membership in American society. By the end of Bolden's career, the music and its people had both emerged into a new phase. The music was by now firmly established, even if it was still largely confined to the New Orleans nonwhite communities. It was no longer just one man's new way of playing but a style, and it was deepening into a genuine tradition. As for the people, they were now loosed, for good or ill, from the last of those special states within which they had existed since their enforced arrival here almost three centuries before. No longer were they property, nor were they the contraband of war, nor freedmen, nor the wards of Reconstruction; nor were they any longer protected by the laws that had been enacted in consequence of all this. They were at last *out*, even if not wholly free.

The relationship then between the state of the music and that of its people is hardly an adventitious one—as Sidney Bechet was careful to point out. Thinking back to this time, he observed that all those who had been slaves or conditioned by the reality of slavery "needed the music more than ever now; it was like they were trying to find out in this music what it was they were supposed to do with this freedom: playing the music and listening to it—waiting for it to express what they needed to learn, once they had learned it wasn't just white people the music had to reach, nor even to their own people, but straight out to life and to what a man does with his life when it finally *is* his."

That is the large pattern within which we can see something of what Bunk Johnson's life and career mean, and so it may not be too important that Johnson probably rearranged some personal history to associate himself with the legendary Bolden. He may well have moved his birthdate back ten years to 1879 in order to make that Lincoln Park date with Bolden plausible, and on the grounds of his feeling for the tradition one feels his right to do this.

Johnson said he was born in New Orleans on Laurel Street, between Peters and Octavia, to parents who had been slaves. There were thirteen other children, so life must have been a struggle. At six he was in school at New Orleans University, one of three black colleges established in the city during Reconstruction. All three had grammar and high schools attached to them, and New Orleans University was distinguished by the quality of its music instruction. Its faculty was among the first to recognize the importance of preserving the old spirituals, and in the 1880s the Original New Orleans University Singers became popular for their performances of those songs that had done much to sustain earlier generations. The school's chapel organist was Wallace Cutchey, and Johnson credited Cutchey with teaching him to read music and to play the cornet. "I come out of New Orleans University in 1894," he said, "and I was fit for orchestra."

By "orchestra" Johnson meant the marching bands that were so immensely popular a feature of the city's life. Almost any occasion would do as the pretext for a parade, the bands stepping along in their smart uniforms, the social clubs sporting their knee-length sashes and spangled emblems, the parade marshals cutting their inimitable steps, and the crowds getting as close to it all as they could. But most of all it was the music: bright, quickening, demanding, and, in the hymns and dirges, filled with soul. It made kids tremble with excitement to hear that music and see the players. If you were a boy, you knew, watching the players, that this was something *you* could aspire to. And even if you were a girl, there was something fine, something proud about watching those men, transformed from draymen and porters, barbers and stevedores, into bandsmen who could *play* that music, who wore uniforms that sported three rows of brass buttons.

They followed the bands the length of their routes, the boys hoping to hold a hero's horn when the parade paused and the players stepped into some corner bar for a taste. Lee Collins, who would one day make a name for himself as a trumpet player, remembered those long, joyous, sound-filtered days, winding through the unpaved streets where the dust whipped into your face, past the cemeteries where in the still, sultry air you could smell the dead, listening to his special hero, Bunk. And he recalled slipping into Funky Butt Hall to hear Bunk play for the roustabouts, pimps, gamblers, and whores, the boy sitting lost and unnoticed behind the bandstand, memorizing Bunk's special sound.

For such as Bunk there was always plenty of musical work, indoors or out, the parades being a sort of glorious advertisement for one's talent. In the days there were picnics to play in the parks or out on Lake Pontchartrain. There were festive excursions on the broad, brown river, and train excursions that left town early in the morning for places like Homer or Breakaway or Thibodaux. There the folks would picnic under shade trees and the band would play until the train whistle blew for home. As the early bassist Pops Foster remembered, it "took a long time to get everybody out of the woods. . . ."

In the evenings there was work for strolling string trios or small bands at lawn parties or at houses where the red lanterns hung up outdoors signaled fish fries. And there were the cabarets, the dance halls, and, if you played piano, the high-class whorehouses. Once, Bunk Johnson recalled, he'd played one of these high-class places himself, joining Jelly Roll there after playing with the Eagle Band on Perdido Street until four in the morning. Then he had gone over to Hattie Rogers' sporting house to play soft accompaniment to Jelly Roll's blues "till way up in the day."

Thus for the players, nights and days ran into each other. When they knocked off at four a.m., they would gather at Pete Lala's saloon at Customhouse and Marais or at 25s across the way. The working girls would join them there for drinks, maybe breakfast. Sometimes they would jam, or else the piano players would take turns while day broke pearlsoft over the city roofs and the market stalls opened with the swish of brooms. If they had daytime jobs, as many did, they would struggle home, hang up their night clothes and put on overalls. Pops Foster told of catching the five o'clock streetcar to the stables: "There you'd pick up your mule team at six a.m. and start for the docks to pick up a load at seven a.m. Once you got your team hooked up and started for the docks, you could sleep because your mules would follow the wagon in front." Sometimes, if you were lucky, you had a helper on your job who could drive while you dozed a little and then wake you to load and deliver. Get off work at four in the afternoon, go home for a bit of sleep, then up on the stand at eight. So now there began to be others like Bolden who could not stand this pace and who burned out like shooting stars, leaving behind little more than the memory of their sound.

What they played was increasingly indigenous, the European dance music becoming secondary to the blues and the ragtime compositions adapted to ensemble from piano. Especially the blues, for this was the sound that came from the inmost core of the Afro-American experience, even further in than the spirituals. The blues was the sound of suffering, but it was also the sound of a creative triumph in the very rush of that suffering. It was a music made up out of old sounds: the horn that had blown the slaves out of bed and into the still dark fields of dawn; boat horns on the river courses; cows lowing; trains whistling; voices calling in greeting or encouragement or simple identification across wide fields; voices moaning in loss, separation, irremediable longing. The true mood of the blues, said the New Orleans pianist Clarence Williams, is "the carry-over from slavery— nothing but trouble in sight for everyone." In New Orleans, if you couldn't play the blues, you wouldn't be hired by blacks for their occasions. They wanted that sound.

And when it came to blues, it was Bunk. There was no other player in town who could get inside them as he could. He seemed, recalled one admirer, to "put his whole heart and soul and mind into each note." The way Bolden had played the blues had been the genesis of his fame, and so it was for Bunk, only with this difference: Bunk was no showman, no shirt-busting star. He played neither for show nor power but for tone and phrasing. Such beautiful tone, they said, such phrasing, such a wonderful ability to play second cornet, filling under the lead with his blue and glowing notes. Here was a musician to emulate, as perhaps one could not hope to emulate Bolden with his huge power. Buddie Petit, a cornetist of local acclaim, once gave Lee Collins a high compliment in telling him, "Your studyin' [playing] put me in mind of ole Bunk." And Collins had replied, "Well, that's my man, that's the guy I'd like to play like, Buddie." Petit had then said to him, "That's the guy I come behind, too, Bunk."

Louis Armstrong remembered Bunk in the same key:

"When I was a kid in New Orleans," he told an interviewer, "Bunk had a better tone than anybody, I think. A genius— played a lot of beautiful blues." Armstrong remembered something else about the man, and this was that he was a hard, hard drinker, known for this among a group of men who used alcohol like liniment. "That story," he said, "that he used to teach me and I used to play with his horn, ain't true. He never had time for us kids—always on the way to or from the Eagle Saloon, where he drank a whole lot of port wine. You could smell it coming out of that horn—but it sure sound beautiful."

Bunk was hardly alone in his habit. It seemed somehow to go with the life, as the Bolden legend tells us. This, the crazy hours, the women, the outlaws and gamblers who were their daily associates; above all, the endless drinking: this is what it seemed to take to play that hard, to get that special drive, to desire to put all your heart and mind and soul into each note. Buddy Bolden, said one old-timer, played like he didn't care. It wasn't that he didn't care about the music but rather that he was heedless of how much his care for it might cost him. This was his own version of "Careless Love." It was almost as if his successors were issuing with their behavior a continuing challenge to the white majority that had spurned Bolden and now spurned them and their music. It was almost as if they were saying, "All right. You say it's whore-house music, jungle-thumping, low and dirty. You segregate it into the District where you say it belongs. Well, we'll live it out on your terms, we'll play our music here for our people in our own way, and we'll *still* beat you." Maybe the truth and experience of the blues had caused them to feel such a triumph was possible.

If there was something like this challenge in the behavior of Bunk and the others, it was fatal for too many. In Bunk's case it cost him his position, first in the Superior Band, then in the Eagle Band, and then in the New Orleans musical world altogether. Pops Foster recalled that Bunk got so bad that he began showing up for dates too drunk to find either the bandstand or his lip when he put his horn up to blow. Eventually he came to spend most of his time inside the Eagle Saloon, drinking and sleeping off his drunks. "He'd drink till he passed out," Foster said, "and then sleep it off on a pool table, get up, and start drinking again. If we came along and wanted to shoot pool, we'd just lift Bunk off and lay him on a bench. He got to drinking so bad that even the Eagle Band fired him about 1910 and no one else would hire him." Foster concluded that about then Bunk left town with a minstrel show and disappeared into the back country for more than a quarter century.

Foster was off a bit on the date of Johnson's departure, which appears to have been around 1914. But his guess is a suggestive one, for about 1910 the tight, cohesive world of the New Orleans musicians had begun to break apart, and men were leaving singly and in groups what had once seemed a place that would be home forever. Indeed, the world of the black South was breaking up. The withdrawal of the flimsy protections of Reconstruction, the implementation of Jim Crow statutes, and the contrasting expansion of Northern industries with their employment opportunities were impelling hundreds of thousands of Southern blacks northward. "Michigan water," sang Jelly Roll Morton, memorializing the exodus, "tastes like sherry wine." And now, "Mississippi water tastes like turpentine."

Some of the players like Bunk had already traveled out to neighboring areas like Alabama or Mississippi. Jelly Roll hit the winding, destinationless road as early as 1903. Tony Jackson, who could range on piano and in voice from opera to gutbucket blues, left around 1908. Bassist Bill Johnson took a band that included the outstanding cornetist Freddie Keppard on the vaudeville circuit around 1911. Then Keppard kept on going with the Original Creole Band, touring the entire continent, having a successful run at New York's Winter Garden, then settling down in Chicago where the band created a demand for more New Orleans groups. Through it all Keppard kept sending back a steady stream of clippings to his fellow musicians in New Orleans. At 25s in the after hours, the men would read these and think about their chances up north.

Then in 1917 the U.S. Navy pressured the city government into closing the District, and this event coincided with a local business slump. There were more incentives now to leave town, and Joe "King" Oliver, generally acknowledged as the biggest star still around, made his plans to go north.

It was not that all the good players were leaving, nor that the closing of the District meant no more work. Maybe at bottom it was nothing but a vague, shared sense that something here had come to an end, that the frantic all-night party of twenty years was at last over. A player looked around him in the early morning gatherings at Lala's and 25s and missed familiar faces. It made him wonder why he was staying on.

So while a good many stayed or else made only short trips out of town while keeping New Orleans as home base, a good many others began lives as wandering minstrels, taking their music into every corner of the country and into foreign lands, some never to return, some to die broken and forgotten in strange places far from the warmth of the original nurturing community. "Do you know what it means to miss New Orleans?" the song asked. The question took on a special poignancy to those whose travels took them ever farther away but who kept in mind those great, unfading days when they and the music had been young and New Orleans was the whole world.

Some went north to Chicago or St. Louis to establish in those places little New Orleans musical enclaves. Some went to California. Others began less adventurously by playing dance music on the boats that traveled upriver from New Orleans. And still others like Bunk Johnson went out with the shows.

The Rabbit Foot Minstrels, the Silas Green Minstrels (a

New Orleans outfit), the Georgia Minstrels, and other troupes employed a good many New Orleans players, packing them along on their grinding schedules with the actors, dancers, singers, and stage hands to play accompaniment for the skits and songs.

There were also opportunities to travel with Wild West shows, where the players functioned as noisemakers, and with patent medicine shows. These latter were small, low-budget, hard-driven affairs, circling the rural routes in wagons, rolling into small hamlets, setting up the stock of nostrums and a rough platform for the little combo. The circuses too employed New Orleans players who wanted a taste of the road, and Bunk once told Lee Collins that he had made a tour of Europe with Barnum and Bailey, that Queen Victoria had seen the show, and that she had fallen into hysterical laughter—a somewhat improbable reaction.

For those like Bunk who left New Orleans but wanted to remain down home the usual thing was to organize a small band and attempt to improvise a circuit of country dance dates. In the tiny weathered halls the local whites would sit on the bandstand with the players, watching the black folks dance or else watch from behind a roped-off spectator section in a reprise of Congo Square days. Sometimes the band might be held over another night to play for whites only. Then they would be off again, looking for that next date.

Out of these years of wandering, 1914–1920, we have scattered word of Bunk Johnson in Baton Rouge, Bogalusa, Lake Charles, and Mandeville. In 1920 and intermittently thereafter until the fall of 1931 Johnson played second cornet in Evan Thomas's Black Eagle Band out of Crowley and in Gus Fortinet's Banner Band from New Iberia in the western parishes of Louisiana. In the early twenties he married Gus's daughter, Maude, but he was still on the road a good deal, in the western parishes and in Texas and Kansas City, a town whose black section jumped to the rolling bass rhythms brought there by musicians out of the Southwest. Oran "Hot

Lips" Page, later a blues trumpet player and singer, recalled a boyhood thrill in Corsicana, Texas, when he had carried Johnson's bag and horn up from the train depot. Just another stop for Bunk, another date, doubtless not remarking much the toothy, big-faced boy who stood staring at him there in the cinders of the depot yard, but maybe grateful to be relieved of his bag for a moment as he made his way to the black section of town and that night's job.

Bunk's association with the Banner Band and with the Black Eagle might have been in some ways almost equal in musical satisfaction to his heyday in New Orleans. This was hardly the big time, of course, for there was little fame to be had in the western parishes and even less money. And out in the country Bunk knew that others of his time had gone on to fame and money—King Oliver in Chicago, little Louis Armstrong eclipsing them all; while others, latecomers, derivative like that Original Dixieland Jazz Band he slyly disparaged in his letter to the jazz historians, had capitalized on that tradition he had helped to make. Still, there were satisfactions of a sort out here. For one thing, playing with Evan Thomas gave Bunk the ideal opportunity to play his restrained, inventive style of second cornet. Thomas, a dark, bullet-headed man, was a player of remarkable power and taste, and many who heard him considered him the equal of Armstrong. At the dances the country crowds wanted blues, and Thomas could drive these out with a fiery intensity that would give the second cornet superb openings for shading and embellishment.

There was another thing out here that was satisfying to a musician like Bunk: in the country the original relationship between the players and their people was preserved. Here were those who truly needed this music. It was low-cost, deeply familiar, and it gave them both release and identification. So here there was that abiding empathy, that vital interchange between players and dancers on which Bolden had capitalized. Perhaps then it is not incidental that Thomas, the leader and drawing card, was said to be an authority on Bolden's career, for both he and Bunk were in a real sense carrying on the Bolden tradition, keeping close to the cultural and emotional basis of the music.

Up North things had changed drastically: the audiences were different with different needs, and Oliver, Armstrong, and the others had accommodated their music to those differences, smoothing and unifying their ensemble sounds, augmenting their reed sections, relying ever more heavily on arrangements instead of polyphonic improvisation, and staying away from the rough, sad blues that had once been the outstanding feature of their repertoires. Such changes could not have been lost on so passionate a keeper of the tradition as Johnson seems to have been, and they might help to explain why he turned down at least one offer from Oliver to come north and join the King, why he seemed to Oliver and others so singular and solitary a man, his motives, artistic impulses, and even his whereabouts almost perversely mysterious. The truth—or at least part of it—seems to be that Johnson was driven by a fierce dedication to his art and its cultural circumstances as he had learned these in New Orleans. He was willing to add new tunes to his repertoire, including the very latest popular favorites, no matter how trivial. But he was utterly intolerant of inferior musicianship and suspicious of anything that smacked of the substitution of a canned performance for the genuine article.

There was also the matter of race relations. To play in the North required an emotional and psychological suppleness, an ability to execute sudden adjustments when the rules were changed and a black musician might find himself treated just as he would have been down South. You had to learn to anticipate such changes, learn when you could afford to be something like yourself among the whites and when you had to assume another guise. Johnson was highly sensitive about race relations, and there was something unyielding and stark in his character. Perhaps then it was better after all to stay South, playing your own way for your own people, where you could always count on the rules.

II

In the first days of November 1931, Charles "Buddy" Bolden died unknown and unmourned in the state asylum at Jackson. In the last days of the month the end came for his devoted successor, Evan Thomas, and, in a way, for Bunk Johnson, too. Bunk had returned to Crowley from Kansas City just in time to join Thomas and the band for a projected tour of western Louisiana, Texas, and Mexico. The band rehearsed through the middle of the month, Johnson the loner living apart from the rest but making the rehearsals where he and Thomas worked out versions of the new hits "Stardust" and "I'll Be Glad When You're Dead, You Rascal You."

On a Saturday Thomas got the idea of getting a dance date for that night at the nearby town of Rayne. That evening the men gathered in back of the small country hall to drink the bootleg whiskey of the local distributor, John Guillory, standing in the mellow gloom of a shed while the crowd gathered out in front. It was going to be a full house, even with such short notice: Evan was always a good draw. Even though the stuff on which they now slugged away was terribly raw, they got enough of it down to want more, and they went next door to Guillory's house to ask for another half pint on credit, telling Guillory that they would pay him back after they had taken up the collection. The man refused but then asked why Evan wasn't with them. He doesn't come around like he used to, Guillory said. Then someone, no one remembered or would say who, told Guillory that while he had been serving time in the penitentiary, Evan had indeed been coming around a lot—to call on Mrs. Guillory. A bit of foolishness here, a slip, maybe an ounce of revenge for Guillory's refusal to trust them with the half pint. That seemed to be the end of it.

Inside the packed hall the band set up, and "Big Eye" Louis Robertson, the pianist, was delegated to take up the collection since this night in the pianoless hall he would not play. Then Guillory was there in front of the low stand, a savage deerfoot dirk tucked in his belt. Surveying the band in a swift and ruthless glance, he came around the platform and up its stairs. Evan, guessing, *knowing*, now what was coming, began to rise, protesting innocence, but he was not quick enough and Guillory caught him on the way up, slapping him hard in the face. Evan leapt frantically behind little George Lewis, the clarinetist, and Guillory had the knife out now, slashing at Evan over Lewis's shoulder. Now Evan bolted down through the parting crowd, making for the dark road outside, and there in the midst of the little hall Guillory caught up with him, slamming his blade through Evan's back with such fearful force it cut a rib in two. Evan cried out once, "Oh, my!" and then ran on instinct out the door and down the road to collapse on a porch as his life drained away into the boards.

Inside there was an explosion of noise and movement, several men struggling with the enraged assailant, the rest of the crowd fleeing, and the band climbing out a window. Guillory got out, too, but then quickly he was back with a pistol. Hiding outside in the darkness, the band could hear the man smashing their instruments, shooting holes through Chinee Foster's drums. Not until Guillory had fully demolished everything and left Evan's and Bunk's horns twisted pieces of scrap metal, did he exhaust his rage, at which point the deputy sheriff arrived to make the arrest.

In the Rayne road were the surviving members of what had a few minutes before been a band, Bunk with his mouthpiece and George Lewis with his shirt-front dark with Evan's blood. They went somewhere and sat around in silent amazement, drinking some whiskey. Then Bunk made some remarks about sticking together and going on with the tour, but they all knew it was no good. Evan had gotten them together, he was the draw, and Bunk had no power to compel a new cohesion. Besides, only George Lewis still had an instrument. So they split up and went their ways, Lewis, Chinee Foster, and Walter Preston going back to New Orleans together, while Bunk went to New Iberia.

So there he was: stranded, without an instrument, his teeth going bad and not enough income to have them worked on, and the nation in the full grip of the Depression. His was a predicament similar to hundreds of other black musicians who in these tough times lost the little they had gained in the twenties. Now they were forgotten by the Northern record companies who had understood that with the influx of Southern blacks into Northern urban areas there would be a market for downhome music and so had recorded the black musicians on "race" labels. Stranded like Bunk wherever unalterable circumstances found them, the players had to put their instruments down and go on to what their people called "the jobs"—those low-paying, unskilled, often hazardous positions reserved for blacks. And they were lucky to find even these.

A few name bands—Ellington, Armstrong, Cab Calloway, and (later in the decade) Count Basie—kept going but only by accepting the terrific pace of endless one-nighters. Remembering those days and the stunning succession of hot nights in nameless places, Armstrong described himself, shower-stall wet, his shoes going "squoosh, squoosh, squoosh"—and still feeling that he had to give his audiences more.

For Bunk Johnson there were few one-nighters. He borrowed a cornet once in a while to play with Gus Fortinet's Banner Band on those few occasions when it was worth it for the band to call a dance. But mostly when he played at all it was tuba, for by 1935 his teeth had gone. The great majority of these days he spent as a handyman, W.P.A. music teacher, truck driver in the New Iberia cane fields, factory hand in the hot sauce plant where they squeezed into bottles the dynamite juice of the Avery Island peppers, and caretaker at a mansion called The Shadows. Here he tended the grounds once carved out and cared for by the vanished slaves whose hands had also shaped and fired the bricks of the big house in which there now resided a descendant of the original owners. This man was both fascinated and awed by his leather-faced, toothless servant, descendant of other slaves, who was by turns charming and witty, then dark and silent, on his dignity.

The year 1937 began with Franklin Roosevelt announcing in his second inaugural that a third of the nation was ill-housed, ill-clad, and ill-nourished—an announcement that surprised no one, least of all the black bands who on their tours had seen it all and had seen it up close. In this year Joe Glaser, Armstrong's manager, had the band booked for another extended tour that included dates in the deep South. In Savannah, Armstrong met up with one of those of whom the president had spoken—Joe Oliver, his mentor, the King, *his* gums gone with pyorrhea, his last band of pimple-faced amateurs dispersed, his touring bus busted in some junkyard, and the landlady holding his trunk for rent. So here was Joe, Armstrong remembered, "He's got so bad off and broke, he's got himself a little vegetable stand selling tomatoes and potatoes. He was standing there in his shirt-sleeves. No tears. Just glad to see us. Just another day." Armstrong gave him what he could afford and the boys in the band chipped in. That night Joe Oliver was in the wings when the band went on, dressed to the New Orleans nines in the clothes he had gotten out of hock: Stetson, box-back coat, high-button shoes. But then the band went on, had to go on, leaving Joe Oliver behind, sweeping out poolrooms and writing letters to his sister in New York in which he mingled his premonitions of death with plans for a comeback. The premonitions were the more realistic, and in April 1938, the King was dead. His sister went into debt to have his body shipped to New York for burial, and Armstrong was at graveside when they lowered Oliver, without music, into a markerless grave.*

A few months thereafter in New Iberia, Armstrong was confronted with yet another apparition out of that New Orleans world he had left so far behind: a prematurely aged, toothless man who came to hear the band at the New Iberia Training School and introduced himself as Bunk Johnson. Pops Foster, then Armstrong's bass player, noticed the leader in animated conversation with the old man and wondered who he was. When Armstrong told him, Foster was shocked, admitting he never would have recognized the man he had known so well in the District days, whose unconscious body he had cleared off the pool table at the Eagle Saloon. "I didn't either, man," said Louis.

And again Armstrong and his men went on, leaving in this place an artist who had once been such an inspiration to them, whose talent had made his name famous among the players of a music-mad time and town. Now he was no longer an artist but rather a day laborer, and in a matter of years it would doubtless be forgotten that he had ever been what he once so supremely was.

Except for one man, in his way as singular and driven as Johnson himself, it might have been a dead end for Bunk, ending his days in the New Iberian cane fields, slamming in and letting out the bright, worn clutch pedal of the truck that backed, hauled, and delivered the long, tough stalks. The man was Bill Russell, a Missouri-born musician and composer, at that time in the early stages of his research on

---

*Salvia Range 16, Plot 66, in Woodlawn Cemetery is still unmarked and constitutes a minor kind of national neglect. Here amidst the tombs of Admiral Farragut, Jay Gould, George M. Cohan, and "Bet a Million" Gates, lie the unmemorialized remains of one of our genuine creative talents. The obliging groundskeeper who located the plot for me knew it as the "Oliver King" one.

the New Orleans phase of the music. Russell kept hearing
the name "Bunk": an old timer he was said to be, one of the
real pioneers, who had played with Bolden and was once
regarded as his legitimate successor. Lee Collins and others
thought he was still alive, but none of them could agree on
where he might be or even what his last name was. So wholly
had this been a folk movement, that there were no written
sources to which Russell and his co-researchers might turn.
In 1938, well over forty years since Bolden had stood up in
front of his first crowds and blasted new turns on the blues,
not a single significant work had been published in America
on what was now recognized as a major form of "popular"
music. The collaborative effort in which Russell was now en-
gaged would result in the publication of *Jazzmen* the following year, but in 1938 there were no guides or blazes available
to American historians.

But if there were no printed sources, there were still the
musicians, and there were enough of them with New Orleans memories to make the search for Bunk Johnson a good
deal better than hopeless. Russell brought his questions to
Louis Armstrong, backstage at a New York theater date. Who
is this man we keep hearing of, he asked? Is it Campbell or
Robinson or Johnson? And Armstrong was able to tell him,
not just that Johnson was the name, but that Bunk Johnson
was now a truck driver in New Iberia, that he had no teeth,
no horn, no hopes. But once. . . .

That was enough for Bill Russell, and within weeks he was
in correspondence with the yet faceless, disembodied name,
letters beginning to come out of that unseen place; letters
carefully scripted in slow, heavy, round characters, letters that
burned in Russell's hand with their urgency, their claims, a
whole depthless vault of history opening in serial as he read
them. "This," the man wrote of his place and circumstance,
"This is a Cajun town and, in these little country towns, you
don't have a chance like the white man, so you just have to
stand back and wait until your turn come. That is just the

way here." And this: "You all do your very best for me and try and get me on my feet once more in life. Now, here is just what I mean when I say the word, 'on my feet.' I mean this: I wants to become able to play trumpet once more, as I know I can really stomp trumpet yet. Now, here is what it takes to stomp trumpet, that is a real good set of teeth. And that is just what I am in deep need for. Teeth and a good trumpet and old Bunk can really go."

Russell saw to it that Bunk got the teeth: Dr. Leonard Bechet made him that "real good set." And Lu Watters, whose Yerba Buena Band in San Francisco was winning an audience with its careful reconstructions of the original New Orleans sound, sent twenty-five dollars with which Bunk bought a battered trumpet and a used cornet which he characterized as "just a little bit better than a coffee pot." Shortly after this, Bill Rosenberg, a young trumpeter and a New Orleans enthusiast, donated his own horn, a good new one, and Bunk played this to the end of his career.

Despite the fact that the home recordings Bunk made with his acquired instruments were terribly disappointing to them, four music historians, including Russell, met in that "Cajun town" where the old master was waiting his turn, determined to record him, whatever his condition and present level of talent.*

As always, Bunk was a surprise. At his house that first evening, the wet lowlands air hanging on the visitors like soaked cheesecloth, the man had shaken his fist at appearances, had shown them his donated horn, pumped its clean, cushy valves, and then played a slow blues, his signature of old, bringing tears to the eyes of the foreign emissaries. When he had finished there had been no question left unanswered in the still after-air other than who might be rounded up in New Or-

---

*"The real Bunk," record collector Ivan Alexander once observed, "probably isn't anywhere on records. It was too late for him, but you can get an idea of how good he must have been by listening to what he tried."

leans to record with this unexpectedly vibrant "relic."

They got a band together at last, Russell and the others hunting through the blue, bleak hours of the city's dives and taxi-dance halls for those old enough to know what Bunk and his art meant, hale enough to represent something of that art in their own present sounds. Big Eye Nelson, the first hot clarinetist and who had been with Bunk in the Superior Band around 1908, was too sick to do. Johnny St. Cyr, who had been Jelly Roll's banjo player, had injured a hand on a construction job. George Lewis, survivor of that murderous night in Rayne, had a loose front tooth he wrapped tight with package paper and a clarinet he held together with wire, rubber bands, and hardened chewing gum, but he could play. So could that lanky trombonist of the old Sam Morgan Band, "Jim Crow" Robinson. He had never known Bunk except as a name, for he had begun his career years after Bunk had gone out with the shows. But they knew one another's language, and Bunk told his sponsors that Big Jim would do fine.

The personnel raked together like bright embers out of the ashy heap when the fire has died, the old places gone or converted to other uses, the great trail blazers dead, and some of them like Bolden and Buddie Petit buried right under this runny soil in unmarked graves—after all this the would-be revivalists still had another barrier. It was the old one, that which had so much to do in the making of the music itself: race. In New Orleans in 1942, there was not a single place to be found willing to lend its facilities to the recording of the black artists who had helped make the city wholly unique. In Bolden's day, white New Orleans had officially ignored him except to record in the newspaper a late, berserk action, and it had also disavowed its paternity of the music, preferring to let any other place take that tarnished honor. So here, with Johnson and the others gathered to record the history of the New Orleans sound, the city, unofficially, was being true to its own narrow sense of history.

Finally, at Grunewald's music store, they found a young man who knew better and who told them they might use a third-floor storage room. There with a tiny home recording machine, the band assembled in June's crushing heat, the windows opened in prayer of breeze but instead the sounds of trolleys, traffic, and dogs filtering in.

Bunk chose a tune they all knew, "Yes, Lord I'm Crippled," and they ran through it once to get the feel. Then Bunk counted off and they went into it for real, Bunk's lead weak but the band filling nicely. Into the second chorus Bunk got going and executed some pretty embellishments, but then his lip gave and he vanished into the thumping ensemble sound, coming back at last for a wavery ride-out.

They tried "Ain't Gonna Study War No More" next; this time Bunk's lead was strong and sustained with some good phrases and a suspended note, not suspended long enough, but the sort of thing that made listeners know something of the talent that lived at least in the old man's mind. Then a marching blues, then a sure-enough march such as they had played in the parades of long ago when the kids who were now grown had followed them through the dust, the horse manure, the flies, and the bright, fluttering sashes of the fraternal marchers.

When they had finished, there was a monument inside the little recording machine and a comeback of sorts ready for Bunk Johnson. They had gotten him, as Armstrong said, out of the fields and back on the stand. This was a justice, though it would prove inadequate to Johnson's long-nursed needs. He was invited for another New Orleans session and then out to San Francisco to take part in the New Orleans revival there. Sitting on his trumpet case in the aisle of the troop-crowded car as the train rattled the southern route west, Johnson was recognized by the black porter, Mutt Carey, once himself a famed New Orleans cornetist whose single recording from his prime preserves for us scratched and fuzzy evidence of all that neglected brilliance.

In California Bunk had his concerts, interviews, air shots, but the New Orleans revival was thin after all, and the man who was to have been a feature of it ended this phase of the comeback as a manual laborer, hoisting oil drums with his stringy arms.

There were three East Coast engagements that picked him up after California, and when Bunk and his New Orleans band played the Stuyvesant Casino in New York in the fall of 1945, the reviews were as enthusiastic as the crowds. There in the long, barnlike room where a chandelier shed a spangling of cheap glamour over the players and the tables of listeners, Bunk and the others were disconcerted by the audiences' reluctance to dance. It was just a bit like being back on the boats or at Southern country dances where the whites would come to gape at the black antics.

The odd estrangement between players and audience was a reminder, if any was needed, of that peculiar, reserved esteem in which the music and its artists were held by the majority culture. These old guys were exciting, all right, astonishingly vigorous. And they were an authentic bit of Americana, especially pleasing to a nation that had just successfully met a fearsome challenge to its identity in World War II. But within the excitement, the adulatory reviews, the applause at the end of each number, there was an affectionate and ill-considered condescension, an unwillingness to try to understand this music and the history behind it; much less to consider the meanings of the phenomenon both players and audiences were now parts of. Armstrong, the smiling ambassador from the all-but-unsuspected world that had nurtured this sound, understood this attitude and its implications, for in his tourings he had met it too often to mistake it. At the end of his life he told of a sage bit of advice given him by Slippers, a bouncer in a New Orleans honky tonk. It was 1922 and King Oliver had just sent for his boy to come up to Chicago and play second cornet behind the great man. "I sure like the way you blow that quail," Slippers had told

Armstrong, "and you going up North now. Always keep a white man behind you that'll put his hand on you and say, 'That's my nigger.'" Armstrong not only followed this advice, but he learned to live with it and what it meant, turning back upon itself the force of white prejudice with his mugging smile. The man was a great artist in more ways than one.

Bunk was not. He could be subtle and witty, but he lacked Armstrong's psychological suppleness. He once remarked that all this "comeback" stuff was a sort of phantasm, since no matter where you might play, how high up you might imagine yourself, there was "always somebody who'll come up and say to you, 'Hey, nigger, play this.'"

He was bitter. Even in the midst of his brief time in lights, he was bitter. It had all come too late. As he told a young admirer at the Stuyvesant Casino, "These are all borrowed notes." And even now he felt misunderstood, underrated, condescended to, a bit of an anachronism, an old-timey colored noisemaker resurrected from a circus world. So he showed off his bitterness, appearing late to dates or not appearing at all, or showing up drunk in a kind of shadowy reprise of his last days in New Orleans when he had drunk himself out of work. He dozed on bandstands, tried to return the insult he felt by playing bad notes, missing changes, suddenly altering tempos. He feuded with his bands, denigrating the men publicly as "emergency musicians," and sulked when Sidney Bechet or Jim Robinson got some of the spotlight's impersonal glare.

When in the last days of 1947 he found himself back in that Cajun town, not many were grieved. Old Bunk had incurred too much resentment, even hatred, with his unspent grudges. He had too much of that "memory thing" Sidney Bechet had said was necessary to play this music. Armstrong probably spoke for many in the New Orleans musical family when he dismissed Johnson curtly for "trying to live at sixty like he did at twenty-five. And man, that whiskey too much for him. Should have stuck to port. Next time you look around, he ain't here no more. Goofed his break. Didn't take care of himself."

This time there would be no rescue. He must have known this as he waited for the end in a frame house on a back street of New Iberia. In November 1948, he suffered his first stroke and then a disabling one shortly thereafter. At the end of the next June, Bill Russell, even to this last Bunk's friend and champion, made his final pilgrimage to the old man, finding him asleep in a chair, his toothless mouth agape, the precious false teeth broken and unusable. Maude Fortinet Johnson tried to rouse her husband into at least some politeness: here, after all, was Bill. But all Bunk murmured was, "There's nothing to talk about."

Russell spent that night on the floor of Bunk's bedroom, listening in the oppressive darkness to the sounds of a neighborhood band, trying to attend beneath these the faint, measured breathing of the man lying so lightly there in his worn body.

In the morning Russell shopped for the family. He shaved Bunk, feeling with a sort of terror under his hand the infantile softness of that once iron lip. Then he took the train out, leaving Bunk there in his last back country blues.

III

Coming out into the country from New Orleans and heading for New Iberia, one gets the impression that the whole southwestern portion of the state is filled now with the hiss and stamp of heavy industry. In the Avondale shipyards, across from which I stopped for gas, there were the vast, mastodonic skeletons of drilling platforms canting up from the marly mud, and everywhere there was evidence of the oil boom that has so transformed life there.

Westward the land is yet in cultivation: long flat fields of rice and beans and cane with rows of oaks riding the borders. In the distances I could see tractors tearing up funnels of dust and dropping white fertilizer into furrows. At Morgan City and Franklin the oaks became mossy giants casting soft shadows on the road and over the elderly houses lining the main streets.

At the crossroads store three ancient black people sat on a bench in the sun, composing a picture that resembled a nineteenth-century glass plate negative. Against a sinking sun two boys trooped the border of a field, dancing some shared experience. Crossing the highway, two girls, buxom in dresses, laughed and shoved each other.

New Iberia was announced by the usual belt of plastic— signs, food, stores. At a gas station I asked a black woman waiting in a car for directions to St. Edward's Cemetery, and as she hesitantly gave them to me two black men emerged from that station, one with his arms held stiffly out from his body, hands half cupped.

"What's this?" he asked tensely, and while I began my explanation, the second, larger man cut me off.

"Maybe you better ask that dude in there," gesturing toward the white attendant we could see in the station window, "and quit bothering this woman." His yellow eyes, narrowed by drink and anger and a thousand small frustrations I would never know, kept my tongue firmly between my teeth, and I thought, walking to the station, of Johnson's letter to Russell, telling him a bit of what it was like to be black in New Iberia: you just have to stand back and wait until your turn come. From the station window I watched those two debating whether to do something further about me, but they didn't, and some few minutes later I was at St. Edward's, a half-block space tucked between neat rows of one-story bungalows.

I walked the crabgrass ways between the mostly anony-

mous concrete slabs. Somewhere among them Bunk Johnson lay, and although there had once been a hand-lettered
inscription on his tomb, it was gone now so that the ignorant
searcher had at last to turn away, baffled and reluctant, sure
only that he had paused near the right place.

Then, through misdirection, I found my way into Bunk's
quarter of town, mean and poor but lived in, with kids playing in the street at the end of which sat the gray clapboard
house, weed-shrouded and shuttered tight against the on-
going world. A man in a watch cap regarded me with interest and a familiar distance as I crouched and scurried,
shooting pictures quickly against a sun already obscured behind trees and buildings. Though his brown uniform shirt
said "Otis" in mechanical script, he told me his name was
George Thompson and that he was the owner of the shuttered hulk I had come far to see. Would you, I asked, pausing to focus from another angle, let me in there? And he
said yes while I tried to explain to him what Bunk Johnson
might mean to me.

The rooms were dank, moldy, crumbling away inside with
none to attend, surely not the teen-agers who regularly sat
on the back porch to drink cheap wine and beer and leave
behind their urine and empty bottles. Sitting on that thin-
planked porch, lost in their own concerns, perhaps, a boy
and girl fumbling at each other would not have heard the
infinite trickle of plaster, brick and lathing from within as
the house gathered into itself like an old person shrinking
into the last silence.

And here were George Thompson and I, moving through
the rooms—sad and small-seeming as they were in their na-
kedness with their wallpaper stained by leaks and drooping
like a widow's flesh. Through his talk of the economic potential of the place, I kept wondering, Which one? Which room
was his last one? Wondering in which flaked, strewn cubicle
the last spark had winked out, the moment seeming ultimate
even to him who had quit so late and so grudgingly. In this

evening gloom, feeling my own mortal pulse and half listening to George Thompson, I pictured that last hour, Bunk's fading light, his assent to the ending of that long road here: to have come back from New Orleans, San Francisco, New York, and Boston to this little town set within its guardian fields and ways, to this back street house that now was falling slowly about what was not even a neighborhood memory of him.

"Notice this," George Thompson was saying in the notlight. "Up front here this house is *sound*. These are old cypress. See the width of these planks? But back here," gesturing toward the rear of the house, "that's new lumber, and it's gone. My wife says to tear it all down, but I've been wanting to save it. Now I guess I can't."

In the fireplace there were flecks and broken angles of brick atop the ancient whisper of someone else's ashes, and I saw Johnson here, waiting with a kind of fatality for history to catch up with him. I thought of him in the 1930s, hearing from this place the indistinct news of a bigger world, waiting for Armstrong to send that promised horn; writing those labored letters about the New Orleans days in which he had truly lived. There had been a *tone* to life there, something never to be forgotten however much of it had been experienced numb with drink and fatigue, his head buzzing with the long nights' sounds and smoke; remembering himself with mingled familiarity and astonishment as he stumbled out of some saloon into the city's sub-tropical morning and offered some spellbound kids a hit of Jack Johnson wine. Then to have waited here for his due while King Oliver toured and Louis made records and posed for glossy stills in creamy coats—"Yours, Sincerely." Then the visitation of the historians to listen to his version of history coming brassy, unsubdued, and strong as taste from the polished bell of the donated horn. All of this was heavily around in the rooms, and I felt his need for recognition and the justice of that need as well as the hopelessness of it.

In the last light I shook hands with George Thompson on

the drooping front steps and thought of Bill Russell's last visit here as I drove away, the house becoming ever smaller in the slant of my rearview mirror until it vanished like unrecorded history.

IV. Memories of Song

Bill Russell rescued Bunk Johnson from what would almost certainly have been a permanent obscurity. In his researches of other early figures like Chris Kelly, the early cornet star who died without leaving behind so much as a single photograph, Russell was not so fortunate. But had it not been for him, even more of the New Orleans musical story would have been forever lost.

Certainly the city itself had scant interest in this dimension of its history when Russell began his fieldwork here in the late 1930s. Like most American communities, New Orleans has been reckless in the preservation of its past. Only within the last twenty years have organizations like the Louisiana Landmarks Association, the Friends of the Cabildo, and the Preservation Resource Center been formed to combat as best they can the mindless rage against the past that seeks the obliteration of everything thought to stand in the way of Progress.*

---

*A recent mayor of the city was quoted to the effect that producers considering New Orleans as a location for their films should not assume that any-

In the matter of jazz, official neglect was more than mindless: it was downright studious. After all, the social origins of the music were not such that the city could take pride in them, a problem recognized as soon as jazz had transcended its local popularity and had been taken to other cities and there exposed to the embarrassing questions of the curious. Thus in the summer of 1917, the *New Orleans Picayune* editorialized that "jass music" (the old, revealing spelling) was "the indecent story syncopated and counterpointed." Like the improper anecdote, the editorial continued, "it was listened to blushingly behind closed doors and drawn curtains, but like all vice, it grew bolder until it dared decent surroundings, and there was tolerated because of its oddity." New Orleans, the editorialist concluded, is interested in jass, but *only* because "it has been widely suggested that this form of musical vice had its birth in this city—that it came, in fact, from doubtful surroundings in our slums. We do not recognize the honor of parenthood. . . ."

The attitude persisted, even hardened in the intervening years. When Russell and the others came to New Orleans in 1942 to record Bunk and the old-timers, the city could take pride in the pirate Jean Lafitte, who had used a Bourbon Street blacksmith shop as a blind for his slave smuggling. But it was not much interested in the art created in the city by descendants of those slaves—as Russell had discovered in trying to find a recording studio. Jazz was tolerated as a traditional part of the city's extensive night life, along with prostitution and numbers, and that was about the extent of local regard for it. By the 1940s the sporting houses along Basin Street were long defunct, and Tom Anderson, once vice lord of the District, was only a metal name plate stuck in the paving in front of his former bailiwick. Lulu White's name was also still in place above the door of her "Mahog-

---

thing would be impossible. "There are a lot of things we'd be willing to do for movie people," he said, "a lot of old things we'd be willing to blow up."

any Hall," but the house itself had been empty for years and would soon be demolished. Some of the old halls where Bolden and his successors had stomped the blues were standing and some of those successors were in town and playing. Picou played occasionally, during Mardi Gras for instance. Big Eye Louis Nelson, the first hot clarinetist, was in failing health but playing background music for B-girls. Kid Rena and a few others worked the taxi-dance halls. But other than such vestiges, about all that remained of the music here was a fast-fading memory of it.

Over the next two decades Russell did much to change public attitudes about New Orleans jazz, both in the place of its fusion and in the wider society. These efforts began with his contributions to the collaborative work, *Jazzmen* (1939), which has a strong claim to being the first serious and comprehensive history of the music published in this country.* (It is still one of the very best.) The chapter Russell contributed on New Orleans music is more than anything else a biographical sketch of Bunk Johnson, for by this time Russell was in contact with Johnson, and the forgotten artist's letters were so profoundly impressive that, although Russell may not have known it then, they were changing his life.

Recording Bunk obviously did change Russell's life. In the process, Russell came to understand what almost no one else did: that here was a major aspect of American cultural history that had been very largely neglected and that might soon vanish on the expiring breaths of those few survivors who had firsthand knowledge of its primal days. That sense of urgency has driven him ever since.

---

*Significantly, the beginnings of serious writing on jazz were in Europe. Robert Goffin's *Aux Frontières du Jazz* (1932) and Hughes Panassie's *Le Jazz Hot* (1934) both recognized the great importance of this art form before American writers did. It was hardly whim that prompted Sidney Bechet to live out his last years abroad, nor was it simply wanderlust that sent such important modernists as Ben Webster and Kenny Clarke into European asylum.

After engineering the Bunk Johnson comeback, Russell plunged into the work of recording as many of the old-timers as he could locate and afford, including, among many others, Jim Robinson, George Lewis, Manuel Manetta, and Frank Amacker. This work included not only capturing their playing styles but also hundreds of hours of their reminiscences, a body of material without which a genuine history of the music's origins would now be impossible. His knowledge and contributions were also essential to the founding of the William Ransom Hogan Jazz Archives at Tulane, the most valuable collection of jazz materials in the world. Beyond all this, he helped reintroduce New Orleans music to the American public through his own performances with the New Orleans Ragtime Orchestra, in which he still plays violin, and through his association with Preservation Hall whose touring bands and recordings have brought the sound of New Orleans to millions over the globe.

For the first time in its history, New Orleans jazz is officially honored in the place of its birth. The New Orleans Jazz and Heritage Festival and the names of sports teams proclaim civic pride in the music. Clarinetist Pete Fountain's jazz show and the bands at Preservation Hall are major tourist attractions. Yet it is characteristic of Russell that he takes no credit for this, preferring instead to draw attention to the obvious claims to honor that the music and its artists have.

Each year thousands of tourists throng through Preservation Hall on St. Peter Street where nightly performances of traditional jazz have been held since 1961. Few note the tall, white-haired man who sits in the entryway talking music, but in a central way what they enjoy here is of his making. Like so many others, the founders of Preservation Hall, Allan and Sandra Jaffe, were inspired by Bill Russell, whom they first encountered more than twenty years ago on St. Peter, where he then ran a record shop. And it was through the Jaffes that I met Russell.

This was in late winter, which does not of course mean the

same thing, in New Orleans that it does in other parts of the country. Still, it was chilly in the narrow entryway outside Preservation Hall, and Russell was wearing a raincoat. Above him a naked bulb shed its bleak shower of incandescence over his white hair and the weathered planes of his face. I waited while he concluded a lengthy conversation about the quality of sound on certain recordings. Then we talked a bit. As the band inside the hall struck up again and the last of the pressing crowd had been wedged inside, I told Russell that I had been brought to the conclusion that if one wanted to start on one's own researches into the city's musical history, he would be the man to start with.

"As long as there's one surviving musician left in town," he responded, "I don't know why anyone would waste their time talking to me."

This was not, as I was to learn, counterfeit humility but instead an expression of the urgency that has driven him for forty years: the insistent sense, sharp as a goad, that history is receding from us, life by life, and at so constant a rate that we cannot hope to catch up with it but only to persevere in the pursuit. Once, he later told me, he was on the trail of what was said to be an Edison cylinder recording of Bolden. Whether the cylinder indeed ever existed he never discovered (rumors of it have tantalized searchers for decades) because the leads petered out in some New Orleans junk shop, where, for all anyone knows, the precious item lay discarded and buried beneath other relics of early modern technology. Or maybe it had been thrown out as worthless even by the junk dealer. Russell had on another occasion rescued a bundle of letters and hand-written scores of Jelly Roll Morton's as they waited for the garbage man on a widow's back stoop, marked with the terminal designation TRASH.

Nor was Russell's response a put-off, as I had feared. He would indeed see me and specified a time when he could do so. At his appointed hour, I walked a street of the Vieux Carré bordering the old District. Here were rows of paint-peeling houses, narrow, long, single-story affairs with rooms racked one behind another in the "shotgun" style peculiarly reminiscent of the tombs of the old neighborhood cemetery wherein the older corpses are displaced farther back in the long vaults by the newer arrivals. Some of the houses were of cypress weathered to the consistency of iron and almost all were graced with the jigsaw scrollwork so popular in the nineteenth century: eaves, lintels, porch railings, all silently dancing together some not quite eternal figure above the intruder cars and buses that prowled streets laid out for carts and carriages.

Russell belatedly answered my buzz, materializing out of a profound gloom with a handkerchief held to his mouth: he was in the grip of one of his asthma attacks and apologized as he led me inward. The contrast between the bright streets and this interior struck me suddenly almost blind, but as I shuffled after what I could only hope was the receding white of Russell's shirt back, the darkness began to take on form, and I became aware that the front room was piled to its high ceiling with cartons, books, and stacks of paper through which we now passed as on a forest trail. Then we were in another, smaller room, and in it I could see more of the massed materials, some of them labeled with names that made my heart jump—"Bunk Johnson," "Jelly Roll Morton," "Jim Robinson." Wedged between cartons and files was a small cot, above it on a shelf a record player, and in a clearing a TV and a folding chair. The windows of a small kitchen beyond brought what light there was, and I stood carefully while Russell brought in another chair, afraid to move lest I break into worthless tatters some bit of history the man had patiently gathered here.

Still coughing, Russell poured himself a bowl of dry cereal for his five p.m. breakfast, sat down, and balancing the bowl on his knee, began to talk without preliminaries.

There may have been something of the performance in what Russell gave me that afternoon. A stranger, after all, had asked for some clues to researching the city's musical heritage, and he had granted an audience. If it was a performance, it was a stunning one, and there was nothing of the show-off about it. Like a West African *griot* who carries the centuries of local history in his head and can recite it on request, Russell plunged from the current moment back into that world he had come to know so deeply, taking us steadily, image by image, anecdote by anecdote, back into the past while the light from the windows faded to a whisper of grayness and then into the indigo of evening through which his disembodied voice cut a strangely somber beam.

Beginning with reminiscences of Jelly Roll Morton, whom Russell had heard in an obscure Washington, D.C., nightspot in the late thirties when the great artist had run through the last of his luck, Russell told in not quite random fashion something of his pursuit of history. Recordings of Morton's music had first quickened his interest in jazz, and in the Washington encounter with Morton himself, Russell was picking up the trail that would eventually lead him to where we now sat, only a few steps from the vanished parlors of Basin Street where Morton had spun out his genius to audiences of madames, whores, and customers waiting their turns.

And then there had been Bunk. Fierce and intemperate as Johnson had been in those too late years of his comeback, I nevertheless came to feel that Russell had developed a genuine love for him as well as a respect for Bunk's mind and talent. Russell recalled, with an impersonal sense of vindication, sitting with Sidney Bechet at a nightclub table during the East Coast phase of Bunk's comeback and hearing the old man suspend all conversation with a quick, burst of playing. Bechet was by then becoming exasperated by Johnson's unpredictable behavior and studiously shoddy playing. Now, suddenly, here was the *old* Bunk, the original Bunk, coming right at them with the attack of an undiminished artist. When it was over, Russell didn't have to say anything to Bechet.

"Oh, *I* know Bunk can play," was all Sidney had said, and it was enough.

Probably, Russell mused, there was an inherent reason why players like Bunk Johnson could suffer eclipses so total that within a few years no one could recall their names. "Their audiences," he said, "the ones who really loved their music, were gamblers, pimps, whores, all sorts of hustlers." Such people got around a lot in their brief lives, but they were not the sorts to spread an artist's reputation or bring him (or her) to the attention of groups other than their own. And when they found their own bleak endings, the memory of a man whose sound had once delighted them would fade a bit more until it would vanish altogether—unless he were fortunate enough to have some indefatigable rediscoverer such as Bunk had in Russell. Too many had not been so fortunate, and to Russell the losses of their sounds and stories were tragedies of history.

Thus, running like parallel streams through his talk, were the laments for those losses and the pleasures of the rescues and discoveries made through the years when Russell worked at his task, a solitary man laboring almost unnoticed at something the nature and scope of which was much beyond general comprehension. Through the darkness and the words flowing quietly, evenly from the unseen speaker, I saw him following the faint traces of Bolden on out of the city to the asylum at Jackson and then back again to a potter's field. Or traveling downriver to inspect the old Magnolia Plantation where some of the early hot players had been organized into a brass band under the direction of a colored Creole music teacher from the city. Or photographing buildings associated with the music's earliest days—pathetic, discarded fragments now, slivered into halves or quarters by subsequent developments with few besides Russell to note them and almost none but he to care about the dark vibrancy they once had housed, the fated aspirations of the players who had bounced their music around those interiors. Someone interested in

the music's local origins ought to visit these sites, he concluded, however altered they now were, for there were few
other ways left to get some sense of the physical world that
had given jazz what welcome it received. Better still, there
were, as he had earlier indicated, a few musicians in town
who had memories of the old days and who might be willing
to share them. He gave names and places, snapping on a
light so that I could write them down, and then arose and
led me back toward the present. I could see a glint of it in
the street light that managed to find a way through the ar-
chival forest of the front room.

Saying a cordial good-bye at his stoop, Russell was hit with
another spell of coughing through which I waited, nervously
aware that so much talk could have done nothing good for
his condition. "You know," he said finally, speaking from behind a handkerchief held to his mouth, "this town is strange.
I remember once coming back here from a trip, and as we
drove over the lake bridge I suddenly smelled it again: death
or something decaying, rotting. I know it's killing me. I keep
saying I'll move somewhere. But. . . ." He shrugged a little,
and the rooms behind him completed the thought with its
burden of obligation.

It was thus I left him, standing there watching the first
stirrings of the city's nightlife, as he must have been doing
for years, with what seemed to me a sort of proprietary interest. Before his gaze pedestrians moved with a quicker beat,
cars swished toward destinations that were not those of daytime, their headlights heedlessly rippling the rows of old
houses; and from the honky-tonk that is Bourbon Street, the
first tentative toots of the city's historic come-on filtered down
the narrow ways and around corners. The old New Orleans,
the inevitable New Orleans, beautiful, tawdry caravansary for
Kentucky raftsmen, Mississippi Valley merchants, sailors,
steamboatmen, soldiers, filibusterers, and now conventioneers
was emerging from beneath its current, evanescent disguise.
The Trade Mart Tower and the Superdome had vanished

from view as if the revenant place had winked them out with a mascaraed eye-lid. On street corners the women would now be taking up their hopeless vigils while in the bars the musicians limbered up. For a moment in this place, past and present came together for me as Russell had made them do, and I turned back to look at him, standing there with his handkerchief in hand, regarding anew the old action.

II

Professor Jim Humphrey sat stiffly, as much as possible holding himself away from the hot wicker of the seat while the narrow gauge train clicked its way south from the city toward where the land extended its last tatters of green into the blue and gray of the Gulf. Beside him on the seat were his cornet case and a used saxhorn. When the train made the stop for Magnolia, Professor Humphrey would climb down and in his swallowtail coat walk the shell road across the low land toward the distant smokestack that towered over everything.

The stack marked the site of the sugar mill on the plantation of Henry Clay Warmoth who had been governor of the state during Reconstruction. When Mark Twain visited Magnolia Plantation in 1882, it was a model of the new, mechanized approach to sugar production with six hundred fifty of its twenty-six hundred acres planted with cane and getting a high yield of a ton and a half per acre. Twain described the fruitful orange groves, the wide and fertile fields, and the great mill that was a "wilderness of tubs and tanks and vats and filters, pumps, pipes, and machinery." Twain had little to say about the millhands, but it was because of them that Professor Humphrey made this trip once a week in the late 90s: he was teaching their children the right way to play brass band music. If a kid really wanted to learn and his parents could scrape together the money for an instrument, Professor Humphrey would purchase one in the city and bring it down on his next trip. More than one such kid, coming in from the fields in the late afternoon, would find that his precious horn had been moved, might even have spit in it: a younger brother had been fooling with it out behind the cabin, trying to raise some sound out of the mysterious smooth darkness of its bell.

But there was no foolishness in the presence of the light-skinned, firmly correct professor. The rough kids in their slouch hats and battered gallus-held trousers were taught the classical approach to their instruments, how to make the "*tu*" embochure, how not to overblow, how to keep the tone precise and clear all the way to the end of a note. And like the other Creole professors, Humphrey used the method of public ridicule to urge his pupils to the high standards his class had always maintained. "Young man," he would say sharply to a wayward or inattentive pupil, "Young man, you have a wooden head." And the others would giggle.

There must have been more good heads than wooden ones down there because eventually Professor Humphrey considered some of them sufficiently accomplished to bring them up to the city in 1900. Sixteen brass pieces, they were "Jim Humphrey's boys," and they marched under the banner of the Eclipse Band, becoming in time one of the most respected of New Orleans's many distinguished brass organizations.

"I could maybe tell you something about the fellows in the Eclipse Band," said Willie Humphrey, grandson of the professor. There was a pause. "But Magnolia, that's before my time." We were speaking by telephone. I had called Willie from one of those corner grocery shops you could still find in older sections of New Orleans—all bay leaves and filé, chicory and beef tongues—a heavy, rich smell with its own story to tell of the city's past.

His voice was hesitant, cautious, and I wondered whether to him I was just another tourist trying for a connection with a colored jazz musician or whether Willie could put the name and voice together with a face. I had seen him play dozens of times with the Preservation Hall Band, traveled with him to a dance date, and once he had given me a driving tour of greater New Orleans. But with the popularity of Preservation Hall in recent years, the older players like Willie and the band's trombonist, Jim Robinson, had become a bit weary of the somewhat naïve attentions of the crowds. Willie after all was then in his seventies, and he had looked into a lot of faces over the end of his clarinet.

Finally, he relaxed a bit, enough anyway to say, "Well, I *might* be able to talk with you sometime tomorrow, but, understand, I'm not sure. You call me tomorrow—but not too early—and I can tell you then." In the meantime, he could give me general directions to Magnolia Plantation.

Though built and flourishing before Willie's time, it was still there, if barely so. State Route 23 wiggles down the east bank of the Mississippi past Ironton, Myrtle Grove, and Pointe à la Hache before it cuts through the lands that once were part of the plantation. There were still productive orange groves on the west side of the highway, but on the east the fields lay fallow except for someone's thin strip of a cabbage patch. The shell road Professor Humphrey had walked ran between stands of weeds higher than a man's head, and through the haze of their slanted stalks you could see the big house surrounded by a few scrubby jack pines and a lonesome live oak. Huge, even in its shrunken dilapidation, its white plastered walls were marred by great scabs, some windows shuttered and others open to the sun and rain. Roof and galleries sagged heavily earthward, yearning toward the weeds. Yet it was not hard to imagine Governor Warmoth dispensing planter hospitality here, especially when you went into the grand foyer and noted the ostentatious sweep of the main staircase.

But the objective here was not the big house, imposing as it so clearly had been. The objective was the sugar mill and the cabins in which the hands and their children, the professor's pupils, had once lived. Of these there was even less evidence. The shell road ran past the big house on into the desolation of the fields until it reached what was now a clearing in the weeds, a wide, level spot littered with fragments of flagging and crumbled bricks. Here, choked to its jagged, broken top with bristling bushes and creepers, was a fragment of the sentinel smokestack. Other equally fragmentary brick structures lay within the rioting tangle of vegetation and stacks of castaway tires and agricultural machinery. Only a single cabin remained, and this doubtless of a later construction than those that had once given some shelter to the mill families.

Waiting, listening for something here, you could hear nothing; even the weeds were silent and motionless in the still afternoon, and the mill site was too far from the highway for you to have heard the zip of traffic. But you could, with some kind of background, *think* of the sounds that once were here. Beneath those of the great mill—the crushing of the cane, the bubble of the vats, and the hiss of steam—there would have been the homely sounds of labor: the creaking of wooden wagons, protests of axles, the dry clack of rakes on the stalks, stamping of draft animals, human voices, talking, humming, whistling. These sounds could help to establish a historical continuum, stretching from the present moment back through Professor Humphrey's time into the ante-bellum days when the basic sounds would have been the same. And this might move you to wonder how substantially the hands' lives had been changed by the war and Reconstruction. The methods of production had changed, of course, along the stretch of the continuum, but what about the daily lives of the workers? In Professor Humphrey's time here, how much wider or higher were the horizons of those who worked these fields and this mill, those who had gazed across the impossible distance that separated the mill from the big house with its nine tall northward windows? Surely in 1895 it would have seemed as far from here to there as it had in 1860.

This situation, evoked by the sounds of those days, is what must be imagined if we are to understand what profound and urgent appeal there would have been in the weekly appearances here of that proper city Creole, wearing his swallowtail coat, encouraging the kids to teach each other toward excellence—kids whose only instruments had been their voices and the cane quills they had improvised from the fields and who would already have observed enough of their elders to know what lay in store for them. Professor Humphrey was an emissary from another world, and the skills he taught could seem a ticket to that other, wider world that lay somewhere up the converging lines of the narrow-gauge tracks. One of the sounds that eventually got into the blues was the sound of the train whistle as it neared where you were and then wailed on out of hearing as it passed you by. But through Professor Humphrey, these kids from the fields and brakes could catch that train and ride under its joyful hooting all the way to New Orleans.

Willie Humphrey's home was in a tidy residential section on the edge of the Garden District. Here there was one small bungalow after another, each with its trim lawn fenced with wire hoops and signs warning you to keep yourself and your dog off. At the intersections of these quiet streets and the main thoroughfares there were the usual ganglia of groceries, Laundromats, and bars.

Willie was there on the porch, perhaps watching the schoolchildren at play across the street, more likely waiting to see who it was he had agreed to talk with. There was a slightly impish grin on his handsome Creole face as I came up the walk toward him, and then he said slowly, "Oh, yeahh. If I'd known who it was. . . ." And we went in.

A distinctive characteristic of New Orleans musical history is how much a family thing it is: not only did all the players know each other and consider themselves a special group from a special place, but many were related as well. Musical families were one of the strongest carriers of the New Orleans tradition, and the Humphrey family takes its proud place amidst the Baquets, Barbarins, Halls, and Tios. So it seemed both easy and convenient to launch a conversation there in Willie's warm living room with a reference to the grandfather and his downriver pupils of long ago.

Like so many in the racial and ethnic gallimaufry that is New Orleans where miscegenation has been a way of living for centuries, the grandfather's father had been a white man. Perhaps for this reason Professor Jim Humphrey's upbringing had been middle class, a part of which was that obligatory musical training. This was training, his grandson insisted, in "*legitimate* music, you understand." Not jazz, that style for which the Professor eventually developed a natural and abiding scorn.

Yet, like the other colored Creole teachers of that time, Professor Humphrey had been powerless to prevent his students from hearing the new music once they had come up out of the country. How indeed in the New Orleans of 1900 could they have failed to hear the new, "ragged" style? Even more: how could they not have been attracted to that style, these black youngsters who had never in their rural lives imagined that one like themselves could achieve *fame* by playing a kind of music that sounded so defiantly native? So, even as they played in the Professor's Eclipse Band, they were beginning to drift off into that other style of music and its life ways.

Chris Kelly was a prime example. Born at Magnolia Plantation in 1891, Kelly had come up to the city to play cornet in the Eclipse Band, but he had quickly picked up the new style and become a part of it, the professor's strictures not availing. A comically careless dresser, remembered for wearing whatever he happened to seize upon around his house—tan shoe, black shoe—Kelly identified himself with the *non-*legitimate players and their Uptown audiences rather than the light-skinned, legitimate musicians of Downtown. He became a celebrated blues player, working the cabarets, halls, and tonks, capable of producing explosions of emotion with his endless inventions on the old country blues, "Careless Love." "He really was something on that one," Willie remembered.

Perhaps inevitably, the new, corrupting style invaded even the professor's family when his own son, Willie Eli Humphrey began playing his clarinet regularly in the Crescent Orchestra about 1913. "My daddy played in the Eclipse for years," Willie said, "but this other band was different." It included the Carey brothers, Jack on trombone and Mutt on cornet, Wiley King, bass, Charlie Moore, guitar, and Tubby Hall, drums. Not much "legitimate" music here. One of their numbers was called "Jack Carey" because it featured loud slides from Jack's trombone. Parts of it they had borrowed from a current quadrille, and some years later it was known as "Tiger Rag," though in the music book of the Original Dixieland Jazz Band it was referred to starkly as "Nigger Number 2."

Here was the departure, for certain, and I could easily infer from what I knew and from Willie's words what the professor would have thought of his son playing all that "rough stuff," that head music, perhaps at an outdoor dance held in a vacant lot of Uptown where they might spread a canvas over the pokeweed and dirt to smother the dust raised beneath the dancing, shuffling feet, the band under lantern light with insects flitting out of the summer darkness past the ends of their horns.

Still the professor persisted in his teaching, perhaps (vainly) hoping that his grandchildren would avoid the pitfalls of the new music. As they came along, he taught them: the grand-daughters, and the grandsons who would follow their father into the new music: Willie James (1900), Earl (1902), and Percy (1905). "We all got good fundamentals," Willie said. "I think he made me a pretty good musician and a pretty fair man. No, I wouldn't say he was exactly mean about his teaching, but he meant business." Here he smiled to himself with what I thought a trace of rue.

Even if a respectable Creole family had been able to keep its young boys out of the District across town (and where indeed the father himself played his music), it couldn't have kept the bands in their advertising wagons out of the home neighborhood, and when they would roll to a stop at some strategic corner to play a slow blues or jazz up a march, you could hear them for blocks. A contemporary of Willie's re-membered how as kids they would be playing at something, and then they would "suddenly hear sounds. It was like a phenomenon, like the Aurora Borealis—maybe. The sounds of the men playing would be so clear, but we wouldn't be sure where they were coming from. So we'd start trotting, start running—'It's this way!' 'It's that way!' And, sometimes, after running for a while, you'd find you'd be nowhere near that music. But that music could come on any time like that. The city was full of the sounds of music." Like Willie this boy later made such music his life.

Of these sounds, so seductive and pervasive, Willie re-membered most vividly those produced by the cornetists King Oliver and Freddie Keppard and by the clarinetist Lorenzo Tio, fifteen years Willie's senior and like him a member of a famous musical family. So here was an extracurricular teach-ing against which Professor Humphrey as well as Professors Chaligny and Nickerson and Cutchey could not ultimately contend. Indeed, the strength of the New Orleans tradition really came out of this system of apprenticeship, the aspiring youngsters listening hard to the accomplished older ones, not learning so much note by note, but absorbing a style and getting a *feel* for how it should be played.* "You listen around," Willie explained. "Steal a little here, steal a little there. Take a little of this and that. You know, it's trial and error. And practice. You can't just get up there and play anything."

This last remark is a reference to the method by which a folk tradition like this is maintained in its standards: by the possibility, in fact the *threat,* of the ridicule of the masters. In New Orleans these older men would leave the stand in an ostentatious display of disgust if some brash player thought he could be up there with them just playing anything. Bunk Johnson remembered the older heads knocking the horn from his mouth when he hit wrong notes. Innovation was prized, to be sure; Bolden's first fame had come on the notes of surprise. Men were celebrated for the changes they could make on the blues, like Chris Kelly. But the surprises and the changes were now securely within the tradition, that is, The Right Way. If you wouldn't—or couldn't—do it The Right Way, some member of the band would be delegated to slip a note under your door. It would read simply: "You are fired."

Willie James Humphrey's apprenticeship to the tradition was served at neighborhood street corners; along the avenues, listening to the bands advertise their talents; at the dances where those talents would be on display; and then under his father who took him to his first jobs: playing violin at the home of a Poydras Market butcher and at a lumber camp near Bogalusa. In 1919 he was in the Excelsior Brass

---

*Here we can make use of an enlightening analogy drawn by Alan W. Watts. Writing in *The Way of Zen* of the differences between the musical training of students in the West and in the Orient, Watts observes that a student in the Orient "learns music, not by reading notes, but by listening to the performance of a teacher, getting the 'feel' of it, and copying him, and this enables him to acquire rhythmic and tonal sophistications matched only by those Western jazz artists who use the same approach."

Band led by the cornetist George McCullum, Sr., but later that year, like a lot of New Orleans players, Willie got the itch to travel north, to see those places—St. Louis, Chicago—everyone was now talking about. "So I went to work on the boats."

Working on the boats meant playing in a dance band aboard one of the big cruisers of the Streckfus Line as it made its calls up river: Natchez, Memphis, St. Louis, Hannibal (a rough place to play, recalled the music's first great percussionist, Baby Dodds), Davenport, Dubuque, La Crosse, Red Wing. Playing several nights at a town, the band would entertain the whites one night, the blacks the next, and sometimes the whites would come merely to gape at the players, for in these places they might never have seen a colored person in a white shirt and tie. For most of them, this would have been their first actual exposure to the new music. Bill Russell, raised just above Hannibal, first heard jazz from a riverboat without knowing what it was. Bix Beiderbecke apparently heard Oliver and Armstrong play Davenport, and one of the many attractive if improbable legends that adheres to his name has him sitting alone at night in a skiff in the middle of the big river and listening to those horns shouting across the dark water.

In St. Louis where the boats would stay two weeks, the talk that late summer of 1919 was all about the Big Town, Chicago. "So many people talking about it," Willie recalled, "I just had to see for myself. So I went to Rock Island and took a train. Not to join anybody, you understand, but just to look around and listen."

There was plenty to listen to there and all of it good downhome music. In the summer of 1919, Oliver had one half the town behind him and Freddie Keppard the other. Willie ended up playing with Oliver at the World Series, and here he got up from the davenport on which we were sitting to rummage out a scrapbook and find within it an aging photo of Oliver and a very boyish Willie in the bleachers at Comiskey Park. "And these," he said, pointing with a bent, brown finger at the figures ranged around them, "were all the gamblers and pimps and hustlers." Of which there had to have been more than a few, for that was the Series the heavily favored White Sox dumped to the Cincinnati Reds.

Willie had also played with Freddie Keppard, the other star of that time and place: the musicians' musician, Jelly Roll's favorite, everybody's all-star. "Freddie had such beautiful tone," said Willie, and I could see his eyes going back through all the intervening years to rescue this legendary figure from that obscurity he had partially willed for himself: approached by the fledgling Victor Company to make the first recordings of the new music, Keppard had either flatly refused or else had done a slipshod job. He simply wasn't interested, though some said he feared that others could steal his material off the recordings. In any case, it was the Original Dixieland Jazz Band that made those first recordings, and they used Keppard's material to do so.

"Such beautiful tone. Good ideas. Freddie played all over his horn. He had a different style altogether from Joe Oliver. Oliver was much rougher, you understand. Freddie was nice and light. Clear. You could be sitting right under him, and it would sound just as nice. But you could hear him two, three blocks away."

That then was the great thing for the Creole players: to be hot, as Bolden had forced them to be, but light and clear at the same time, like their complexions. They wanted to hit those notes *right,* the fingers of the Creole masters like Manuel Perez and Morton delicate but firm on the valves and keys. So one remembered Willie gently fingering his clarinet and coaxing from it an evening bird's song on "Just a Closer Walk with Thee"; and his brother Percy with his unmistakable bright, clear tone that sounded equally fine in the first row or at the very back of a hall.

But here in mid-thought, talking of Keppard and Tony Jackson, another player of this caliber, Willie pulled his head back from that barrel of memories I'd asked him to dip into. Again that slow, slightly impish smile spread across his face. "Listen," he said, "this could go on for *days*. Are you writing a book or something?"

III

It is a curious fact, and one full of significance, that so much of this history is oral history; some might call it "folklore" and others, less friendly, "hearsay" or mere speculation. No one can definitively say what Bolden and the first bands sounded like or even the prime Bunk Johnson. Historians got interested in the spirituals as a result of the Civil War, but half a century later they were not interested in the folk art of New Orleans's nonwhites. By the time they had gotten interested about thirty years had elapsed, a very long time for their informants to have carried precise memories of vanished sounds and vanished players.

The first recordings of the New Orleans players come out of the 1920s, the "Jazz Age," two decades after the sound had been new. Even these were not made by artists still playing in more or less native surroundings but by those who had left home in search of wider opportunities and who found that they had to adapt their music for Northern audiences. And by the time the colored bands got before the microphone the Original Dixieland Jazz Band had already created an unfortunate kind of market for jazz recordings with their million-dollar hit, "Livery Stable Blues."

"Livery Stable Blues" was a derivative, hoked-up version of a number Freddie Keppard used to do. It is suggestive of the ODJB's regard for the music they so successfully commercialized that they should have emphasized the barnyard effects that to the original players were merely occasional jokes. When Keppard was feeling good, recalled his contemporary Mutt Carey, "he'd get devilish sometimes and he'd neigh on the trumpet like a horse. . . ." That was for laughs.

Freddie was a good-time guy, and Sidney Bechet always believed it was for this reason and no other that he didn't jump
at the Victor Company's offer to make those first recordings.* But Keppard did not live in the memories of Carey
and Morton and Willie Humphrey because of his trick effects, his occasional neighs and whinnies. "Freddie had a lot
of ideas," said Carey, "and a big tone. When he hit a note
you knew it was hit." He could play anything, he continued,
sweet or hot. "He'd play sweet sometimes and then turn
around and knock the socks off you with something hot."
Buster Bailey who played with both Oliver and Armstrong,
concurred, remarking that Keppard "could play as soft and
as loud, as sweet and as rough, as you would want." The
blues singer Alberta Hunter, herself a forgotten artist until
she made a comeback in her eighties, wondered why Keppard wasn't mentioned more often in histories of jazz. "You
know," she mused, "he doesn't get the credit he should get."

At this late date it will be impossible to give it to him. By
the time he recorded in Chicago in the mid-1920s, Keppard
was already well past his artistic peak, though in age he was
but in his thirties. The man who was called "King" in New
Orleans after Bolden's demise was, like the original King, a
hard liver as well as a hard player. He punished his body
with huge gouts of whiskey and in Chicago was reported
consuming as much as a half gallon of bootleg booze every
day. At one point he kept a water bottle of it strapped under
his arm for use on the bandstand. After a full decade of this,
Keppard had lost his edge. He could still play with his famed
power, but his execution was often ragged, and by 1925 he
was just another player.

It is a wonder then that Keppard sounds as good as he
does on the few recordings we have of him. On "Stock Yards
Strut" (1926), he is right where legend would have him,

*Some believe he did make them but that they were too "hot" for the mar-
ket Victor had in mind. In the Victor files there is a listing for an unnum-
bered test recording made by a "Creole Jass Band" in December 1918.

strongly out in front of his group and filling every space in the music with the right notes, just as Jelly Roll had remembered. A few months later he recorded "It Must Be the Blues" and left behind at least this echo of the early New Orleans blues. If this was how Bolden and Bunk Johnson drove them out, their local fame is no surprise—or accident. Yet even on these recordings there are flaws: on "Stock Yards Strut" there is a bad fluff where Keppard goes after a high note and doesn't get it, and on "It Must Be the Blues" the ends of some of Keppard's lines sound thin and unsure. But this and a few photos are all the documentary evidence we have.

Talking of Keppard and other early artists one afternoon with the trombonist Jim Robinson, I mentioned that I had come across a "Louis Keppard" in the phone book and wondered if this might be a relative. "That old man!" Robinson laughed, slapping his octogenarian's knee. "Why, he lives back in there somewhere." He gestured vaguely outward from his chest. "Used to be on Villere [Vill-r-ee]." Indeed, Louis was a relative: Robinson said he was Freddie's *older* brother.

Here, surely, was a find, but on Villere no one I asked knew of Louis Keppard or where he lived. In a corner bar, blue-lit and thumping with jukebox music, a man turned from his beer, breathed on me, and told me he thought there was an "old musician" who lived in a yellow house across from the school.

Persistent knocking on the door there, however, failed to produce any answer, except from the other barrel of the double shotgun house from which two small black girls emerged to stand on the common stoop and stare at me. Waiting, indecisive, even beginning to turn away, things went through my head: wrong house? too late? dead in there? and what of the propriety of the visit in any case? After a lifetime of being Freddie Keppard's brother, maybe he no longer wished to answer the knocks of an inquisitive stranger.

Then, slowly, the door opened to the shadows, the late afternoon sun, and the stranger already on the steps downward. There at last was the old man, his face not so much wrinkled as worn, his forehead and nose a polished blonde like old brass or good leather buffed over and again. Liver spots had gathered near the dark eyes in which little or nothing appeared to register, and his spectral-seeming head was thrust forward toward the sound of my hurrying voice. When I had finished trying to justify my intrusion, Louis Keppard smiled slightly, turned carefully, and led me in, holding one hand out from his side as if not trusting in the ultimate insentient compliance of the objects he knew so well.

In the rooms he apparently wanted to show me votive candles fluttered like drowning moths in their oily pools of incense, and Catholic iconography glinted and stared from the walls. Looking at it all, the barrenness of the rooms, trunks sealed, doors closed, I felt myself in the presence of one who had taken to heart the counsel of apocalyptic preparedness and who was packed up and ready to go.

And yet, nearing ninety and all but blind, Louis Keppard had not lapsed into a comatose state waiting for the end. His voice was as high and constant as a rusty fiddle. His hands fluttered up and outward from his lap as, sitting in a high-backed chair close by the heater, he dispensed the graces of his parlor. The gestures compelled me to take in the room with its far wall plastered with photos faded to sepia, the curling, yellowed business cards of musicians, and old news items, all of these tattered, aslant, trailing back into other days. In the midst of the display was a photograph of Freddie, staring, solemn-eyed, his youthful face already swollen with the drink that would kill him. Beneath this on a bench a tuba lay in repose, its solid, serpentine body scored and dented by the edges of trolleys, trains, and a hundred parades.

As he talked continuously and in the upper register it became apparent that Keppard had been expecting someone else, either his guardian (a woman who worked across the street at the school) or a young man from England. It was hard to tell which since he mentioned both simultaneously, though several sentences later it seemed likely that it was the latter. "I was about to give up on him, you know, and put this horn away. We play duets, you know, him on clarinet." This prompted him to cross the room, pick up the tuba, and shuffle slowly with it back into a farther room. I hesitated, not knowing whether he was now indeed putting the horn away, but on impulse I followed.

Keppard sat on the edge of his bed, the big horn cradled by frail arms in shoddy, checkered flannel, but in the moment he adjusted himself to its demanding contours he was transformed from an old man in an empty house into an artist. There was now something right, natural, and *inward-seeming* about the attitude of those arms as they found the worn brass of the instrument. Then fingers touched valves, head bent away in concentration, and deep sounds emerged, so deep I could feel them coming up from the floorboards into the soles of my shoes. The sounds coalesced into the tuba part of "Just a Closer Walk with Thee," the player's breath occasionally issuing too from the big bell, and in the otherwise perfect silence of the room with its robin's egg blue walls flecked with icons I could also hear the thinly padded valves click down and rise again under the square and spidery fingers. In the light of an unhoused bulb the white stubble of the player's sucking and puffing cheecks sparkled like snow crystals. His feet patted a regular measure in their string-tied slippers.

Pleased by my easy identification of this first number, Keppard went into "The Sheik of Araby" and was again gratified and surprised by the featureless stranger's grasp of his repertoire. Then it was "T'aint Gonna Rain No More," beginning with the tuba statement and then a vocal with his fingers tapping the valves in accompaniment: "They used to do that way." He laughed to himself, shouldered his instrument again, and played "You Made Me What I Am Today," then sang this old sentimental song of failed love, and I joined him in its last lines so that we ended up almost together: "It's the curse of an aching/breaking heart." " 'It's the curse of an *aching* heart,' " he corrected me gently.

There was a silence in the dank room as maybe Keppard thought about what to play next, or even what to do next with the stranger, and I broke into it with a question about his childhood, hoping to lead from this into Freddie.

The boys' father had been a New Orleans man and a cook in the Vieux Carré until his early death around the turn of the century. Their mother was from St. James parish ("That's up the line somewheres"). Louis was the first child, a year old when Freddie came along. From the beginning there was music in the house, and at an early age Louis was given a guitar and Freddie a violin, the mother taking them about the neighborhood to play for friends. "She had one in each hand," Keppard recalled, " 'cause we was no bigger than this [holding his hand about four feet above the floor]." Was it true, I asked, that the first tune they learned to play together was "Over the Waves"? Louis Keppard laughed and closed the burnt bulbs of his eyes while he hummed a bar in answer. Pausing a moment, he hummed something I didn't know. "It's 'Just Because She Made Them Goo-Goo Eyes.' "

The recollection of these sounds of other days took him back into them without any further prompting, for suddenly he was talking of the little Keppard boys who had outfitted themselves with shoeshine boxes and worked the Basin Street trade in order to get in on the action of the District. Wearing long pants so as to avoid immediate detection as underage kids, they lugged their boxes and rags from corner to corner, doing their own kind of hustle on the grown-up sports, pimps, and gamblers who would pause to get a shine on their Edwin Clapp brogans: "We'd shine the front, you know, give 'em a lick and a promise. Then we'd hit that box—*pop!*—to tell 'em it's all over. Never shined the heel where they wouldn't look.

"At first, policemen would chase us out of the District, you know, 'cause it was a sporting district—what they now call 'red light'—and them women was sporting right in the street. So, we'd get chased off one corner and run on to the next. They'd hit us with the straps of their clubs." He shook his head in emphasis, the cords of his neck straining. "Nowadays, a policeman hit someone, he'd be a dead issue." I thought then of the young Jelly Roll Morton and his friends, fleeing the District into which they'd sneaked, with the vengeful cop, Fast Mail Burwell, on their tails, slashing at their thin brown legs with his billy straps. "He was known to be Fast Mail," said Jelly, "because he had two legs and feet that couldn't be beat, and he would take the straps on the ends of his club and cut our legs to ribbons."

But for such boys it had been worth the risks, the cops, the District's tough guys, the family disapproval. Morton's family had eventually kicked him out when they found he was playing in a sporting house. The Keppard boys' mother "didn't think too much of this music" until "she seen us in those [band] uniforms, then she was proud."

There was another sort of risk that had to be run. This was getting up your nerve to ask a favorite player for help with your playing. In the case of Louis Keppard, an aspiring guitarist, he had approached Willie Santiago and Bud Scott, the latter of whom had played briefly with the Bolden band. It was rough, he said, asking those fellows for help, afraid to be turned aside, or, worse, of proving unworthy of their attentions.

Like many another string player, Louis Keppard also learned the brass instruments, for this is what it took to get the parade jobs. He played alto horn and tuba with the famed Tuxedo Brass Band, a ten-piece outfit put together around 1910 by Oscar Celestin and including Alphonse Picou, by this point apparently accustomed to the style "without notes." A year later Louis Keppard said, "I had my own orchestra."

This was the Magnolia Orchestra, for a while the regular group at Huntz's and Nagel's cabaret on Iberville in the very midst of the District. From across the way at Billy Phillips's you could have heard the wide-ranging attack of the man they were then calling "King," Louis's younger brother. The Magnolia's cornet player was Joe Oliver who would succeed to Freddie's title when the latter went on the vaudeville circuit, but there were other contenders, too, and within the compass of a few crowded squares you could have heard the competing sounds of Manuel Perez, Bunk Johnson, and Oscar Celestin. Despite the grotesque conditions there was perhaps more creative excitement within these few blocks than there was anywhere else in America at that time, and if the artists themselves could not have made the comparison, they nevertheless felt that excitement, felt they were caught up in something powerful and compelling.

Thus, no matter how old, battered by life, even embittered by neglect a man might subsequently become, if he had lived through this period—and survived it—he would remember it forever with a peculiar intensity. Often, the early players in their reminiscences give one the impression of those who have been in a great race and who afterwards are both exhilarated by the memory of it and spent by the lung-busting effort it demanded. So now Louis Keppard seemed to me as he thought back on those nights-into-days when he and the Magnolia men had played from their hearts "for two dollars a night and tips." And the tips? "Tips? Oh, seven, eight, nine dollars a night we'd divide up between five, six, seven of us. 'Course, with the high cost of living nowadays, that would be different. But in them days you could buy a pound of beans for five cents."

Still, for an eight-to-four a.m. job this wasn't much, though most places would throw in a few drinks. "They give you just enough to give you courage to play," Keppard said. "After that they wipe the slate clean. Then, the next day, you might have a picnic to play. So you go home, take a bath, and then catch Smoky Mary [the local train] to Spanish Fort. Play nine to six for two, three dollars. Oh, I've seen some *hard* days. Hard days. . . ."

This is the hardness that one meets so often in the history of the music, the hardness that so wearied the players then, that broke too many of them too early, that fibers the memories of their days. It all had to come out of *them*, it seemed, out of their hearts and hides, too—everything made up, improvised. The only support they had came from within that strange, cut-off community of underworld people of which they were willy-nilly a part and for which they provided the musical accompaniment. Outside it they had no standing or recognition. They were "bums" or at best itinerant minstrels, carrying their songs from one District to another—St. Louis, Chicago, Harlem—songs sucked up into the smoky air of the dingy dives of their patrons. When disaster came, or disease, or death, it found them mostly alone: the piano player who livens the lives of the girls and their customers in Mobile, as Jelly Roll once had, has to move on until one day he can go no farther, and the road ends. So it did for Morton, friendless and all but forgotten, in the make-believe city of Los Angeles. So too for Freddie Keppard, a wasted hulk in Cook County Hospital where none knew that once he had been a musician. The list is endless.

"When they called up here," Louis Keppard was saying, "to ask where to ship Freddie, I told 'em, 'Don't send him back here: he been gone so long from this town don't nobody know him anymore.' He belonged to the union, they could bury him right where he was." The fixed, slightly Oriental eyes of the younger brother, consigned thus to a permanent exile, stared out at us from the photo on the wall, but Louis Keppard's vision of them had to be an inward one. Moved by an unspoken association, he picked up the tuba once again and showed me how to get those necessary slurring sounds into your playing, ending with a long, brassy whinny. Laughing, he pulled away from the mouthpiece and spoke toward the photograph: "Freddie. . . . He did that way."

V. A Music
of the Streets

In our world a folk tradition is a perishable thing. If we could discuss one in isolation, we might find it has a kind of natural history which, of course, must have an end of sorts. Inchoate, disparate through undetermined time, its forces gather to a recognition. Its earliest practitioners, unaware they are so, find each other, find themselves in each other's work. Something is born then, a special way of doing things, and those who have truly learned it are the masters who will instruct the generations of apprentices.

When such a tradition is created within a literate, nontraditional culture, one that lives by mechanized communications media, it will not be too long before the practitioners of that tradition are challenged by the competing ways of the wider society. When printed matter, educational texts, then radio, phonograph, and finally television bring the news of ceaseless change to the community that fostered the tradition, those within become ever more aware that theirs is not the way of the world that surrounds them. Thus the challenge. Sometimes this can be partially resisted: the Cajun people of western Louisiana and the Pueblo tribes of New Mexico are two familiar examples of folk cultures that have been able to preserve some of their old ways while surrounded by modern America. More often, as has been the case in southern Appalachia, traditions wither away as the younger people, who in time would have become masters, seek to fall into step with the rest of the world as it comes to them daily in schools and through the communications media. Their elders may keep to tradition, stubbornly resisting change, but even they will change slowly, mostly because of their very efforts not to do so. At last a tradition, surrounded by modern ways and cut off from its nurturing roots, hardens into an archaism, a museum artifact, and when the last of the masters dies, the authentic tradition dies too, for there are no apprentices to carry it on.

How finite, then, must the life of the New Orleans musical tradition have been from the first. Created in the very midst of the most modern nation on earth, it grew and flourished in neglect, meanwhile developing a genuine system of apprenticeship. By 1915 this system had produced a distinctive sound, a canon of tunes, and recognized standards of musicianship. Then the players began leaving town, the New Orleans sound gained exposure, and the forces of the wider society began to be felt. Joe Oliver, that tragic and symbolic figure, learned early that what he had played in the District had to be toned down a bit when he traveled out St. Charles Avenue to play white dances at Tulane University. He learned to smooth out his sound even more for Chicago nightclub dancers, and still more for New York audiences. By the end of the 1920s there was little left in his playing to suggest the hard-hitting bravura horn that had earned him his reputation. His band specialized in sentimental fox trots, and other bands had successfully commercialized his best numbers like "Sugar Foot Stomp." By 1930, the New Orleans style seemed dated, for the music it had created had evolved and evolved in other directions. Those who had learned in the New Orleans tradition but who wanted to stay in music had to play along with the trends. Others—less versatile, less supple, stubborn?—kept playing the old way and took the consequences. By 1950 the contrast between the new bop players and the New Orleans survivors pointed plainly toward the end of the tradition. Jazz had become the "tradition of the new" (to use Harold Rosenberg's felicitous phrase), and New Orleans music was an anachronism fated to vanish as a living style when the last of the old-timers passed on.

By the early 1960s even casual observers of the popular music scene had become aware that the tradition's remaining days must be few. Jazz funerals became a symbol of that mortality and so began to take on a sort of circus quality quite distinct from the authentic festive dimension they had always had—a dimension that came out of the West African custom of ancestor worship, where to send off a relation without hired musicians, singing, and feasting would have been an unthinkable sacrilege. Indeed, in my case it had been the chance encounter with a jazz funeral on my first trip to New Orleans that had reawakened my interest in the music. Moving through the streets with the throng, the second-liners twirling parasols and cutting steps, the elderly bandsmen playing their apparently unwearied way through block on block of the ritually circuitous route, you were almost *forced* to wonder: How much longer can this sort of thing last? Later, in conversation with Oscar Henry I felt it could not endure much longer.

It was shortly thereafter that I conceived the idea of working up a tape-recorded autobiography of a traditional New Orleans musician. For all the great players to come out of this city we have scarcely a handful of full-length autobiographies, and my view was that the more we could get, the better our chances of understanding the cultural significance of the tradition, its place in our common history. I made several stabs at this project over the next couple of years, interviewing in brief various players. Perhaps I was searching for *the* right subject; perhaps I was only screwing up my courage to ask someone to commit himself to so major an investment of time and privacy. However it was, eventually I could see no one so remarkably suitable as Jim Robinson, the featured trombonist with the various bands at Preservation Hall. Robinson was friendly, even ebullient; he was certainly old enough to have direct ties to the tradition; and his open, big-toned playing spoke of one of the happiest aspects of the city's musical heritage. I asked him one night at the Hall if I might call on him at home. He agreed, cheerful and casual as ever, and the next afternoon we sat in the front room of his St. Philip Street home, the tape recorder picking up the sounds of clinking glasses and the random street noises that sifted in through the open door. There was a bottle of I. W. Harper and a mixing bowl full of ice cubes and talk of old bands and their players, styles, and of his own style and musical philosophy.

The project was thus well begun, but it was never completed. Over the succeeding years I got down to New Orleans whenever I could to interview Robinson, but over that same span of time it became clear even to me that Jim wasn't interested in this work. It also became clear, to my surprise and delight, that he enjoyed my company, so that eventually the visits came to be just that, and I never bothered any more to bring the recorder or the camera.

In those days Jim's wife, Pearl, was still alive, and the three of us would sit in the close, immaculate living room with the heavy plastic slipcovers of the chairs and davenport rustling when we moved, the walls covered with crisped brown photographs of musicians and bands with which Jim had played. Above the television there was a large photo of a young and strikingly handsome Jim with his horn held aslant his chest, looking casually conscious of his youth, looks, talent: the player in his prime. The picture served as a combination reference point and standard joke, useful to date something from, to measure aging by, or to suggest his ways with women.

Our talk was of such random things but especially of the past—into which I still tried to lead him. He and I would drink slowly, and Pearl would content herself with an occasional beer. Sometimes she would disappear into the recesses of the house and emerge later at the far door of the bedroom to tell us she'd fixed a meal which we'd then eat at the kitchen table—red beans, rice, and hamhocks, maybe.

When properly warmed Jim would play some of his favorite recordings which usually had to compete with the seemingly eternal *American Bandstand* the grand-niece Tammy attended on TV. He would point out particular passages he wanted me to listen to, especially his own ("Just listen to what I do here: some of these fellas, all they can play is melody!"), and after one of these that roused him he would strike his knee with a long, limber hand and wag his head in affirmation, gold-capped teeth sparkling out of the Indian-wide face.

Gradually, in this no longer systematic way, Jim's life details emerged, the rambling talk striking here and there against some fact of place, name, or time. In such a fashion I learned one evening that Jim's given name was Nathan, and that "Jim" was a shortened version of a boyhood nickname, "Jim Crow," some old joke, maybe, that even he had forgotten.

That boyhood was spent about thirty-five miles downriver at Deer Range Plantation where Nathan Robinson was born on Christmas Day, 1892. I had always planned to sometime rent a car and drive Jim down to his old home until one day he told me it wasn't there anymore: the big river had washed it all away. His father had come down there from Richmond, Virginia, perhaps as early as the 1870s. There he met a Louisiana woman, married her, and stayed on to work as a teamster and breaker of mules and horses. Jim recalled trailing the plantation's dusty roads and paths behind his mother, using her long dresses as both handkerchief and security blanket; recalled too the omnipresence of the mules and horses and tack his father worked with; and, of course, the river the other kids would swim in. "I never could swim," he laughed. "Other boys, they'd say, 'Do this-a-way, Jim.' But I'd go right to the bottom like a stone." What schooling there was he had here, and though I had seen him sign his name in a slow, neat hand, I came to suspect that he was illiterate.

There was another, more native, sort of schooling to be had there, however, and this was the music of the country bands. Deer Range was just up the river from the old Magnolia Plantation, and on Saturdays Jim and his friends would go down there to hear Professor Humphrey's boys play a dance. Once he scoffed at me when I confused Louis Keppard's Magnolia Orchestra with this rural outfit that had thrilled him in his youth. "Naw, naw, naw," he said, flapping his hand dismissingly at me. "This was a *country* band. Man, I'm tellin' you, them fellas was *tough! Hogs!*"

One of Jim's three brothers played valve trombone in such a band, and Jim told me he had started on that instrument, though on another occasion he remembered that he'd really started on guitar. In either case, what seems important is the strength of the influence: there was the music right there in the parish and there were immediate models for those who aspired to play it.

In 1910, like a lot of country kids, he came up to the city. Here the music was in its most gorgeous effulgence, dozens of good bands, each with outstanding players, reputations in the making, and more work for a player than he could easily handle. Yet in all this Jim Robinson had no part. In those days he was a longshoreman and might have remained one had he not entered the army in 1917.

In France, where his segregated unit worked at building and repairing the roads of war, "They was some fellas was gettin' up a jazz band, you know. And they needed a trombone. Well, I had been foolin' with my brother's trombone—back in the country my brother had a trombone, but it was a valve trombone and this here was a slide. Trombone is a tough instrument. It's a guess instrument.

"Anyway, he [the band leader] says to 'em, 'We'll take Bob here'—he called me Bob—'and we'll teach him, and he can play the trombone parts.' " So, while the band practiced at a YMCA building, Jim would practice by himself on a slope behind it ("They didn't want me around playin' all them bad notes") until he could get along in the ensemble unnoticed.

"Pretty soon, maybe two, maybe three weeks, I was doin' pretty good. Six weeks, why, I could play right along with 'em. We'd have a special car, the back all fixed up, you know, like a truck, with a red cross painted on the side, and we'd play all over." Then, lowering his voice conspiratorily, he winked at me: "Nurses travelin' with us, too."

In 1919, when Jim got back to New Orleans, the great flowering of the music was barely past. Many of the big names like Keppard and Oliver and Morton had gone north; others like Armstrong were out of town on the boats; and others like Bunk Johnson were drifting into the country. The District that had provided so many jobs was closed. Still, it was a fine place for a musician and would have been called "great" were it not for the scale of comparison. Indeed, there were so many accomplished musicians still in town that Jim hooted when I asked him once whether on his return he had started in playing with some local group. As he subsequently explained, he was far from good enough to cut it in New Orleans, and so he went back to work on the docks. But still the music called, not only from all around him but now also from within. He had the taste of brass in his mouth, and when the time came for the call to play, he was ready with his response.

"I was livin' then down on Marais and Iberville, and I could hear them fellas playin' trombone right next door. When I was on the day shift, I could come out at night and just sit on my back porch and listen to them fellas playin'—*dat-dat-dat*—in that hall. Sometimes I'd sit out there all night long

and listen to 'em play, and I'd think, Shucks! I could do that!
I could do what they doin'! Sometimes they'd play till six in
the mornin'.

"Well, my sister—I was livin' with her then—my sister, she
got this player piano. You ever seen a player piano? Got all
them great big rolls on it? Well, she got this player piano,
and when I'd be on the night shift, then during the day I'd
just sit there and work them pedals and figure out the trombone. And that's where I learned my stuff.

"I'd come home seven in the mornin', sleep a little, and
then get up and just *work* that piano and figure out the trombone. Sometimes my sister, if she was at home, she would
pedal for me."

The call came from Kid Rena who needed a trombone on
an advertising job. Jim's friend John Marrero, who played
banjo in the band, brought Jim around so that Rena could
audition him. The leader was surprised and impressed, and
when the band played later that day at a street corner, Jim
remembered that someone had gone to the house of the regular trombonist, Maurice French, with some bad news. His
voice rising higher toward laughter, Jim reconstructed the
message: "He say, 'Maurice! Maurice! You better come out
here. They's a new trombone player, Maurice, and he sound
real good!' Maurice, he come out to see who was playin' that
way, and if he thought he was sick before, you should have
seen him when he seen me!!"

That was the breakthrough. Rena used Jim occasionally
thereafter, as did the Tuxedo Brass Band, so he was now a
member of the fraternity, even though he continued to work
regularly as a longshoreman. Then he wholly entered it by
joining the Young Morgan Band led by the trumpet-playing
brothers, Isaiah and Sam Morgan. Any time I wanted to get
Jim really talking, all I had to do was to mention either the
country bands of his youth or the Young Morgan Band.
"Ohhh," he would say of the latter in something between
laughter and a shout, "them fellas was a tough band!" He

said they were known as the " 'Time Band,' 'cause our rhythm was so good." Once, he said, the Time Band had been on the river, playing for a day's excursion when they had come alongside another boat with its band going full tilt. First he was serious as he set this scene for me, but then he fell into laughter as he told how quickly his bunch had played the others down. And "them boys that had hired that band, they called out over the side at us, 'Young Morgan Band! Young Morgan Band!' After that they didn't want no other band: 'Young Morgan Band!' "

Here there is supporting evidence. The Young Morgan Band, recording as "Sam Morgan's Jazz Band," made some records for Columbia in 1927. It is indeed a tight, tough group that swings as hard as Jim remembered.

After Sam Morgan's death in 1936, the band disintegrated and Jim gigged around with other groups, mostly in New Orleans. He was still at this when history, in the persons of Bill Russell and Bunk Johnson, found him. Jim was an integral part of the Johnson comeback and the subsequent revival of interest in New Orleans music. He worked regularly with George Lewis's bands in the 1950s and after the Jaffes opened Preservation Hall in 1961, he was a staple of the groups assembled there. Allan Jaffe's announcement that "Jim Robinson will be here tomorrow night" rarely failed to elicit a thrill of anticipation in the hall, and Jim just as rarely failed to deliver.

Thus when I first met Jim Robinson he had more than half a century of playing behind him and an even more remarkable amount of music and life within him, in his laughter, his delight in the ridiculous, in his easy, flowing talk. Some of this seemed to dwindle when Pearl died unexpectedly—though at her age of seventy-six, what can truly be unexpected? It was a different Jim I visited thereafter, and I fancied I could even hear an older, chastened quality to his playing. He was given sometimes to dark moods in which he seemed to huddle within himself and from which not even a stiff glass or two of I.W. Harper could release him. For some time after Pearl's death he continued to speak of her as an active presence. "I get into bed at night," he said once, "and I lie right in the middle. I know Pearl, she around, and this way, if I lie in the middle, she have to squeeze in on one side or the other." And sometimes when the mood struck, he would kiss a heavily retouched photograph of her as a young woman.

For a while Pearl's sister, Viola, came over often from Slidell to help out and keep company, and once I had a magnificent fried fish dinner she fixed, during the course of which I had to make two beer runs to the corner market. But then she stopped coming, and Jim was at home alone a good deal, though his relative Joe was around when not working. Many nights Jim would sit alone behind shuttered windows and bolted door, listening to his music, sipping a glass of whiskey, and going to bed at first light. Occasionally neighbors would visit, especially children, and on warm days Jim, sitting on his stoop beneath a green awning, would be the great-grandfather to the block, waving to the children, laughing at their roller-skating mishaps, pointing out to them a brightly painted mural of himself on the wall of the building facing the vacant lot wherein they played.

And of course the work at Preservation Hall still took him out. Here in the tiny, airless hall, with its splintered floor and massed, sweating tourists, and on the tours the band made throughout the states, he was still the irrepressible crowd-pleaser, the clown, arms flapping, bony butt stuck out, moving in his pigeon-toed circle dance to someone else's solo.

The edge to this act was that he could still play, the crowd's delighted laughter to be followed in the preserved order of things by its admiration as he followed his dance routine with some wide, swinging solo, deep, tremulous reworking of a hymn, or spirited ensemble work, the long slide of the horn glinting out and down, the face intent and wholly serious behind the mouthpiece. Now he was beyond the crowd, his talent and his dedication to it taking him as much out of reach of laughter as of admiration, the artist here entirely himself. This was Robinson's ultimate salvation, this allegiance to his talent and to the tradition within which he exercised it. It was what saved him from both the adulation of his late career and the periodic neglect he had experienced in earlier years. It was, as I finally came to understand through the years of our friendship, that inward place where he truly lived.

II

On a soft May afternoon in 1976, the history of the New Orleans tradition and the symbol of its passing converged for me in a phone call. A friend's voice on the other end told me of Jim's obituary in the day's newspaper. The funeral was scheduled for the next morning, and as I tried to absorb this news, I could see the sun already well spent in the hills of western Massachusetts. I wondered how I could possibly make it. I wondered, too, about the propriety of making it at all. In the eight years I had known Jim the funerals of New Orleans musicians had been attended with ever-increasing outside pressure to the point where they had almost become media rumbles. Recognizing this situation, Louis Armstrong had decreed the simplest of services for himself, and when he died in 1971 no jazz was allowed. If I went, I would become part of the huge scene certain to ensue. And yet I had to go.

The next morning I walked St. Philip Street up out of the Vieux Carré, beginning to pick up the signs of festivity as I crossed Dauphine. Already, well beforehand, a large crowd was gathered outside Jim Robinson's house. Across the street lay the unfinished park, a mess of dried mud, weeds, and boards with a vacant enclosure just opposite the house where they plan someday to erect a statue of Armstrong. And behind the park, there were the remains of Congo Square with its grand Spanish oaks brooding over the spot and writhing their heavy branches like black snakes over that stretch of ground where so much of this music's history sank roots into American soil. Many a time after the intervening houses had been torn away in another ill-conceived "renewal" project, Jim Robinson and I had sat in the shade of his stoop, chatting and looking across toward that bit of green where once the transplanted Africans had danced and drummed the history of their blood. I never knew how much of all that Jim Robinson had ever heard, his interest in history being rigorously selective.

The day even at so early an hour was already steaming up with opalescent clouds hanging heavily about an unforgiving white sun. Beneath this colors matched the heat. Umbrellas of various shades were already unfurled above bobbing heads, not only black and red ones, but striped and parti-colored numbers that looked as if they might have been gotten up for just such occasions. The crowd's clothing suggested more a fair or a ballgame than a funeral.

Around the corner St. Claude Street was jammed all the way to the funeral home, but these were neighborhood people who had merely stepped out of doors: sleepy-eyed drinkers; clots of chatting women with children at their knees; old men with hands in their pockets and faces shaded with straw hats; teen-agers flitting on bicycles through openings in the crowd. A festive air was on a decaying neighborhood Jim Robinson had not seen too much of in his last years. It had become too hazardous now for an old man who might be presumed to have some money on him. As his late wife had once observed, "If you go away without somone to watch, they liable to just run a truck right up to your door and take everything."

Farther on toward the funeral home I came upon a mountainous man leaning against a car with a pair of crutches, their tops padded with torn sheets, resting against his belly.

It was Fats Houston, once grand marshal of these parades and whose jazzy, mincing steps and solemn mien I had seen at the head of that funeral procession on my first visit to New Orleans. Now he was clearly but a stranded observer, and shaking his hand I noticed its missing fingers. "They taking us old-timers out, one by one."

In the parlor of the Blandin Funeral Home, as well as in the streets, there was a festive feeling. Laughter tumbled out, there was much visiting between the rows, and watchers singly or in pairs sauntered casually forward to view the body and just as casually returned to their talk and their plans. Meanwhile, right in all our faces the coffin was propped on its formica catafalque. Under all this buzz Jim Robinson lay squeezed into his box.

Too old to have close living kin, Robinson was attended in this by relatives through marriage: his grand-niece, Tammy, and her father, Joe, who had for the past three years lived with Robinson and had taken on the household duties. There was also a cousin, George, a big, square ex-trucker, now slowly dwindling back into what Big Jim himself became in time— one whose frame was a sort of echoing reminder of old power.

It was hard to tell whether Jim was the victim of a poor mortician's work or of the terrific, wasting disease that took him so quickly. But this clay-colored mummy in gabardine with a wilting rose on what once had been a chest looked like nothing I'd ever known. Especially the lips, sealed and grim like an alien slash across the visage: no lips like those could ever have caressed the mouthpiece of a horn and made it sing.

The finishing touches were an American flag folded into a triangle and propped on the rough pillow at the coffin's head; a floral wreath at the foot with gold letters on a red field spelling FAMILY; a floral cross at the right; and at the left another arrangement in the shape of a trombone ("Preservation Hall"). Behind the coffin hung a large portrait of Jesus.

In the warm and humming room images of Jim and moments with him came unbidden and heedless of their chronology as I gazed at that estranged face or turned away to watch the plaster scallops climbing the heavily painted walls. Then the floral tributes were withdrawn with the inescapable brutality of such ceremonies by two dark messengers in stiff hair and suits, and the lid came down on Jim Robinson, lying now with the flag folded across his chest.

Outside, everything was ablaze, and as the coffin made its careful, jerky descent to a hearse all but swallowed by the crowd, one of the bands, instruments resplendent in the dented and scored glory of many processions, bellowed above the street sounds, "Just a Closer Walk with Thee." As the last of those within emerged into this larger scene, a professional mourner materialized from within the building's innards, adding her broken, runny-nosed lament to the density of sound: "Ohhh, Jeees-us! Ohhh, Jeees-us! Have mercy! Have mercy, Jeees-us!" The mercy at hand was to move beyond this and into the wake of the slowly toiling hearse that seemed almost to sweat beneath the hundreds of hands that caressed its passage amidst them.

Here in the streets was that inevitable confrontation with the world that had done much to render these funerals quaint. Recording devices of varying degrees of sophistication bristled in the sun, and their operators fought each other for position. They seemed about to outnumber the locals as we picked our way through a landscape of glittering glass, burned mattresses, and wasted clumps of cement in weed-grown lots. At every corner turned things coagulated, the backward-walking technicians, the attendant crowd, and the two bands fused yet more tightly as they circumnavigated the old frame buildings with their scrollwork, their crowded stoops, and the dark faces peering from darker doorways that led back from all this light and play.

Our way to the church ended on the strains of a second rendering of "Oh, What a Friend We Have in Jesus," one of several hymns associated with Jim Robinson. Again at the entrance to the church things were tangled and messy, and it was only by a certain brutishness that I got into the building at all. Much of its space had already been assumed by the photographers, soundmen, tourists, and others out for the holiday this provided, and while the coffin was brought in and set up and its lid lifted one more time, the accompaniment most obvious was the measured whirring and meshing of camera gears.

Against a wall at the front three ministerial presences confronted and counterpoised all this with black-capped severity and vestments that seemed out of another, more coherent time. In support of them and of the disposition of the coffin, the organist struck heavily into "Amazing Grace." The majority did not know the words, so that articulation was at first slow and confused but then surging inevitable as a tide, and as the last notes rolled, one of the three dark presences approached his bulwark. Mounted behind it, he took up his incantations just where the sung cadences ceased.

Asking a lengthy mercy for Jim Robinson, he then gave way to the one whose words had ushered the coffin out into the streets, and as this exchange took place the ancillary sounds rushed in to fill the space: people pushing to get in at the doors, muttered altercations, and the unawed talk of spectators at a public event. But once the smallish, skull-capped man had attained his stride this babble was stilled by the menace of his tone.

Sweeping the back of his hand downward toward the coffin, he warned us that he would not repeat the eulogies of last night's wake with all its useless talk of "Robason and what a good man he was. All that"—again, the downward, dismissive wave—"can't do Robason any good now." And here his voice dropped down a bit:

"Last Sunday I had the privilege of attending Brother Robason at Touro Hospital. He wanted to tell me something,
but the voice was too weak. *The voice was too weak.* I baptized
him in the name of the Lord." Sensing then the right moment, a temporary vulnerability in even this audience, forced
to ponder the existential crisis he had raised into view, he
shot home his bolt:

"*Don't* make the mistake Robason made!" he thundered,
dropping the "Brother" now. "*Don't* wait! God won't be played
with!" And then again, finally, "All this won't help him now.
He can't hear it."

On this he turned to the last of the ministers, an ancestral
figure who had patiently endured the shots of the cameras,
impervious to their flickering nuisance. He was the church's
pastor, the Reverend Arthur James Alexander, and as he
arose and stared a long moment at the crowd there was a
sudden hush. He looked like God's inevitable judgment.

This hush—awe, amazement, curiosity—lasted into his
opening words which were borne on a voice as dry and raspy
as sifted cinders, but then the ground noises rose again, ob-
scuring all but the barest outline of message: ". . . raised
together. . . ." ". . . Jim Crow. . . ." ". . . a promise made
more than fifty years ago. If he died first, I would bury him.
If I died first, he would see to my burial." Then, signifying
that he was here fulfilling that promise, he looked in the
direction of the coffin and seemed to speak of Jim Robinson's late redemption and its efficacy, his voice rising and
filling out on the last words, ". . . because He has never
failed, *and never will fail!*" On which affirmation the other
two ministers escorted him back to his seat, from which he
stared hard and sightless beyond the buzzing crowd.

Jim Robinson's harsh assessor now for the third time assumed command and introduced the final speaker with the
preliminary admonition that his speech would be "about two
and a half minutes." In fact, the address of the hip young
minister went considerably beyond that, and though it ran

into clichés, as all such addresses must, still it was heartfelt and knowing, and his voice broke as he remembered Jim's singing of "Bye and Bye." The master of the ceremony relieved him here and guided the audience into the hymn, which began to lilt just a little, as if in involuntary tribute to the man who once so joyously sang it, accompanying himself with a waving white handkerchief.

The respite was brief: our Jeremiah insisted once again on the grim necessities, and where perhaps the service might have been deflected into a group sing, instead he commanded those who would view the body once more to assemble and file past. Whipped by the scorn of his voice and its terrific judgment, we followed one another under his eyes. There was nothing more or less to see than before, and I took this opportunity to escape the remainder of the service.

This was short enough, for I had barely wedged my way out through the crowd on the low wooden steps before a pallbearer emerged behind me, crying at the crowd, "Won't you let the body out? Please! Make way for the body!" Murmurs among us, "Make way," "Make way," "The family. . . ." "The family. . . ." ". . . family. . . ." A path opened and teen-aged Tammy, tearful and uncertain on high platform shoes, and Joe, his hand on her back, passed down it and into one of the limousines. Then the coffin again, borne atop the crowd and lowered amidst umbrellas, heads, shoulders, out of sight until an obscured flash of metal told us the hearse door had closed. The bands, already hushed twice by the grand marshal, now struck up once more into "Just a Closer Walk with Thee," and Jim Robinson had gone on to the last stage.

Once more the cortege took up its wearisome way, inching through the crowd and the tumult, both considerably augmented since the funeral home. Lost in this push and unwillingly carried along by it, I could not even touch the hearse with its dark cargo behind drapes. I was one of those the limousine-borne mourners glanced out at, somber-eyed now and perhaps justly offended by this motley show of strangers who in their turn stared in at them—curious, vacant, suppositious. The car with Tammy and Joe passed me, and in another few minutes the one with Jim's cousin, George, his eyes masked by sunglasses.

The procession moved now through the outer edge of the old Downtown area, past the ranked houses, past the bars and barbecue shacks. The glass-seeded streets sparkled wickedly, dogs barked, and empty cans rolled into the gutters, kicked aside by a thousand scuffed and shuffling shoes.

We were bound for the entrance to a freeway. There the cortege would at last break loose of its shambling retinue, scoop up one of the bands for a graveside service, and hurtle through asphalt isolation five miles out to a newer cemetery on the Airlines Highway where Jim would lie next to Pearl. In the old days the entire procession would have gone all the way to the graveside and then returned with the hot, purgative notes of "Didn't He Ramble" and "South Rampart Street Parade" washing through them. But in those old days there weren't cemeteries five miles out from the center of town, nor were there automobiles to take you there.

We followed as far as we could, but as the freeway entrance loomed and the long cars swung up it, the crowd broke and eddied, uncertain now that the feature attraction was about to be taken from them. But there was yet another band and a "second line" to be formed, and in a few minutes resolution replaced uncertainty and the parade began to generate its own power. With umbrellas waving, the crowd turned back into old Downtown.

I went on alone toward the ramp. Breasting the last buildings before the arid expanse of the freeway, I saw the cortege ahead, balked, stalled, still within reach: one of the limousines had broken down—vapor lock, perhaps. Its hood yawned upward like a patient with a toothache, and I could see that the hearse too had stopped and opened its doors for ventilation. Hot delta sunlight invested the butt of Jim's coffin. Powerless as ever to efface this last misery, I turned back. In the darkness of the overpass the parade raged and swirled.

Notes

The Story Behind a Sound

Perhaps the best general work on jazz is Marshall W. Stearns, *The Story of Jazz* (New York, 1956), which supplies necessary historical and cultural background, particularly for the formative years. Frederic Ramsey, Jr., and Charles Edward Smith (eds.), *Jazzmen* (New York, 1939), was a groundbreaking work when it appeared. As such, it has been somewhat superseded, but it is still one of the best. Two recent works are of interest, though both presuppose considerable familiarity with the subject. Dan Morganstern, *Jazz People* (New York, 1976), is gracefully written and bountifully illustrated with Ole Brask's photos; it contains a valuable annotated bibliography. James Lincoln Collier, *The Making of Jazz* (Boston, 1978), is very good on the technical aspects of the music and includes interesting discussions of the lives, struggles, and achievements of the modernists.

On the New Orleans phase of the music, Alan Lomax, *Mister Jelly Roll* (Berkeley, 1950, 1973), takes up the line of research begun in *Jazzmen* and beautifully evokes the world in which jazz was born. Samuel Charters, *Jazz: New Orleans, 1885–1963* (New York, 1958, 1963), is a useful guide to the colored musicians and bands for this period. Martin Williams, *Jazz Masters of New Orleans* (New

York, 1967, 1979), is now the standard work on the technical achievements of the early players. Gunther Schuller, *Early Jazz* (New York, 1968, 1977), is deeply informed on the technical aspects of the music, and Schuller ventures here some provocative judgments on the sounds of the first bands. It is not for the faint-hearted.

R. Murray Schafer, *The Tuning of the World* (New York, 1977), is a brilliant discussion of the role of sound in our lives. I drew on this work in my opening remarks.

A History of "Hot"

In reconstructing the world into which jazz came I have relied heavily on John W. Blassingame, *Black New Orleans, 1860–1880* (Chicago, London, 1973, 1976). Blassingame's focus here is not music, but his careful depiction of social conditions does much to make clear why this new music would have met with the reception it did—both in the colored communities and in the white. Dena J. Epstein, *Sinful Tunes and Spirituals: Black Folk Music to the Civil War* (Urbana, Chicago, London, 1977), is excellent on the musical customs that were the background for jazz. Henry A. Kmen, *Music in New Orleans* (Baton Rouge, 1966) surveys nineteenth-century white musical customs in that city and gives a few tantalizing glimpses of black musicians who gained a certain sort of local fame decades before Buddy Bolden. The period photographs of George François Mugnier as contained in John R. Kemp and Linda Orr King (eds.), *Louisiana Images, 1880–1920* (Baton Rouge, 1975), greatly helped me visualize that time and place I was thinking about. Here are the bootblacks, the roustabouts, stevedores, and street vendors who found the new music so compelling and so native.

For the legend of Buddy Bolden the earliest published source of substance is Ramsey and Smith (eds.), *Jazzmen*. In Lomax, *Mister Jelly Roll*, the legend is filled out in the vivid reminiscences of Morton and his contemporaries. Nat Shapiro and Nat Hentoff (eds.), *Hear Me Talkin' To Ya* (New York, 1955), adds further memories of Bolden by those who knew him or knew of him. Donald Marquis spent several years tracking down all available historical evidence of Bolden. *In Search of Buddy Bolden* (Baton Rouge, 1978) contains all that we are likely to ever have on the historical figure.

For the early years of jazz and the emotions that went into the creation of it I know of no document more profound and poetic than Sidney Bechet, *Treat It Gentle* (New York, 1960). If the English historian Maitland is right in observing that the essential matter of history is what people thought and said about events, then this autobiography would be the place to begin an understanding of what this music meant to those who created it. Unfortunately, Bechet died before he could complete this work.

Very few landmarks associated with Bolden remain. Funky Butt Hall and Globe Hall have long been gone, and the Longshoreman's Hall on Jackson has now been demolished. Perseverance Hall, however, has been restored. The barbershop on First Street is still in operation, and Bolden's home at 2309 First Street is occupied. Donald Marquis, the preeminent Bolden authority, has been trying to persuade the city that the home be made a landmark.

Herbert Asbury. *The French Quarter* (New York, 1936, 1974).

George Washington Cable. "The Dance in the Place Congo & Creole Slave Songs," *Century Magazine* (February, April, 1886; reprint, New Orleans, 1974).

Samuel Charters. *Jazz: New Orleans, 1885–1963.*

Maya Deren. *Divine Horsemen: The Voodoo Gods of Haiti* (New York, 1970, 1972).

Melville J. Herskovits. *The Myth of the Negro Past* (Boston, 1941, 1958).

William Jackson Meyers. "The Syncretism of European and West African Influences In the Music of the United States." Master's Thesis, Midwestern University, 1962.

T.A. Osae, S.N. Nwabara, A.T.O. Odunsi. *A Short History of West Africa, A.D. 1000 to the Present* (New York, 1968, 1973).

Robert Tallant. *Voodoo in New Orleans* (New York, London, 1946, 1971).

Bunk's Back Country Blues

The two living persons who know most about Bunk Johnson's life and career are Bill Russell and Paul A. Larson. The former has all the materials and background knowledge for a full-length biography, including his lengthy correspondence with Johnson. But he has so many other projects already begun—including books on Jelly Roll Morton and the New Orleans musical style—that it appears doubtful he will get to this one. The latter is not by trade a historian, but he has carefully collected and sifted a mass of Johnson material and has compiled a detailed chronology of Johnson's career. The best extant account of Johnson's life is in Tom Bethell,

George Lewis, A Jazzman from New Orleans (Berkeley, Los Angeles, London, 1977). Bethell is particularly good on the "lost" years when Johnson was in the western parishes of Louisiana. *Bunk Johnson and His Superior Jazz Band* (Good Time Jazz M-12048) preserves the June 1942 New Orleans recording session that launched his comeback; it includes a Bunk monologue on his career. No recorded examples are known to exist of Bunk in his prime. The best examples of his work during his comeback are probably the records he made for Bill Russell's American Music label, but these have long been unavailable. *Bunk Johnson, 1942–1946: The 'Purist' Issues* (NoLa LP6) and *Bunk Johnson and His Band* (NoLa LP3) are inferior recordings in every way, but they preserve some of Bunk's comeback efforts. *Sidney Bechet Jazz Classics*, 2 vols., (Blue Note BLP 1201, BLP 1202) include selections on which Bunk is featured, and on two slow blues, "Days Beyond Recall" and "Up in Sidney's Flat," one can get some idea of what once made him so famous a blues player: there is a lot of heart in those notes. Thanks to the efforts of Bill Russell there is now a handsome marker on Johnson's grave in New Iberia. His house has been torn down.

Sidney Bechet. *Treat It Gentle.*

John W. Blassingame. *Black New Orleans, 1860–1880.*

Samuel B. Charters. *Jazz: New Orleans, 1885–1963.*

Harold Drob. "A Pilgrimage," *The Mississippi Rag* (September, 1979, 6–7).

Larry Gara (ed.). *The Baby Dodds Story as Told to Larry Gara* (Los Angeles, 1959).

Frank Gillis and John W. Miner (eds.). *Oh, Didn't He Ramble: The Life Story of Lee Collins as Told to Mary Collins* (Urbana, Chicago, London, 1974).

Paul A. Larson. "Debunking the Bunk," *The Mississippi Rag* (December 1979, 5).

Alan Lomax. *Mister Jelly Roll.*

Donald M. Marquis. *In Search of Buddy Bolden.*

Richard Meryman. *Louis Armstrong—A Self-Portrait* (New York, 1966, 1971).

Frederic Ramsey, Jr. and Charles Edward Smith (eds.). *Jazzmen.*

Gunther Schuller. *Early Jazz.*

Austin M. Sonnier, Jr. *Willie Geary "Bunk" Johnson* (New York, 1977).

Tom Stoddard (ed.). *The Autobiography of Pops Foster, New Orleans Jazzman* (Berkeley, Los Angeles, London, 1971, 1973).

Martin Williams. *Jazz Masters of New Orleans.*

Memories of Song

My first formal interview with Bill Russell—and the one from which this reminiscence is drawn—took place in March, 1974. I spent the rest of that trip to New Orleans following up leads he had given me. The next spring I visited Magnolia Plantation and interviewed both Willie Humphrey and Louis Keppard. At this writing Russell and Humphrey are hale and active. Willie is now eighty-one. Louis Keppard, ninety-four, has been placed in a rest home.

The method employed in this chapter was to use the interviews as a foundation from which I could illustrate the persistence of memory, memory of art, of neglected achievements. All interviews are structured, of course, either by the designs of the interviewer or those of the subject—or both. Here, obviously, I have drawn on additional materials only passingly suggested in actual conversations, though I hasten to remark that wherever I quote the subjects directly, I add nothing to what they said.

For the section on Bill Russell, I also drew on Mary Cable, *Lost New Orleans* (Boston, 1980), for a sense of how much more besides musical history has been neglected and destroyed in that city. The *Picayune* editorial referred to there appeared under the title, "Jass and Jassism," June 17, 1917. The best survey of the New Orleans jazz scene in the 1940s is Tom Bethell, *George Lewis,* though occasionally Bethell's judgments strike me as needlessly provocative. Nonetheless, this is a rich book, as I have previously indicated.

For the section on Willie Humphrey, the starting points were Bill Russell and Samuel Charters, *Jazz: New Orleans, 1885–1963,* the latter containing discussions of Professor Humphrey and his pupils. George F. Mugnier's photos in *Louisiana Images* were again helpful here in reconstructing the nineteenth-century world of black farm laborers and sugar-mill hands. Henry Clay Warmoth, *War, Politics, and Reconstruction* (New York, 1930), is not very informative on the life of his plantation, but it is at least an entertaining document and ends with this charming disclaimer: ". . . I was never a 'Louisiana Carpet-bagger,' though I might, in the common parlance, be termed a 'scallawag.' " Al Rose and Edmund Souchon, *New Orleans Jazz, A Family Album* (Baton Rouge, 1967), will give the searcher an excellent idea of how vital a part families like the Humphreys have played in the history of the music there. Tom Stoddard (ed.), *The Autobiography of Pops Foster* and Larry Gara (ed.), *The Baby Dodds Story,* contain fine reminiscences of what it was like to work on the boats as

Willie Humphrey did in 1919. Willie Humphrey has recorded extensively, especially over the last twenty years with the Preservation Hall bands. "Bill Bailey," "I Ain't Gonna Give Nobody None of This Jelly Roll," and "The Bell Gal's Careless Blues," *Sweet Emma the Bell Gal* (Preservation Hall 5001), are especially fine examples of his work.

There is not, as I have suggested in the text, a single extended treatment of Louis Keppard's once-famous brother, Freddie. Nat Shapiro and Nat Hentoff (eds.), *Hear Me Talkin' To Ya,* contains the reminiscences of Mutt Carey, Buster Bailey, and Alberta Hunter. Other tributes are found in Alan Lomax, *Mister Jelly Roll,* and Sidney Bechet, *Treat It Gentle.* Keppard can be heard on two currently available albums: *Freddie Keppard: 17 Rare Selections of the Finest Jazz Cornetist of the 1920s* (Herwin 101); *New Orleans Horns: Freddie Keppard and Tommy Ladnier* (Milestone, MLP 2014). Thanks to Chicago journalist Glenn Sheller I have obtained a copy of Keppard's death certificate. It lists his occupation as "Unk." To the question, "Was injury in any way related to occupation of the deceased?", the coroner answered, "No."

Frederic Ramsey, Jr. and Charles Edward Smith (eds.). *Jazzmen.*

Mark Twain. *Life on the Mississippi* (New York, Toronto, 1883, 1961).

Martin Williams. *Jazz Masters of New Orleans.*

A Music of the Streets

As I have indicated in the text, my association with Jim Robinson lasted from 1968 until his death, May 4, 1976. Bill Russell has collected through the years considerable material on Robinson, and there are tapes of Robinson in the William Ransom Hogan Jazz Archives at Tulane. Fortunately, Robinson was extensively recorded in the 1960s. The best of these are the Preservation Hall recordings, *Sweet Emma the Bell Gal* and *Jim Robinson and His New Orleans Band* (5005). Center Records, *Jim Robinson and His New Orleans Band* (CLP 8), has spirited work on it, including a performance of one of Buddy Bolden's favorite tunes.

Martin Williams has assessed Joe Oliver's career in a number of places. The chapter "Papa Joe" in his *Jazz Masters of New Orleans* is a good place to start. The late Oliver can be heard on *King Oliver in New York* (RCA Victor LPV-529, Vintage Series); compare this with *The King Oliver Creole Jazz Band* recordings made in 1923 (Olympic Records 7133).

For Afro-American funeral customs see the good survey of David R. Roediger, "To Die in Dixie," *Massachusetts Review* (Spring, 1981). Also, Georgia Writers' Project, WPA, *Drums and Shadows: Survival Studies Among the Georgia Coastal Negroes* (Garden City, 1972); Melville J. Herskovits, *The Myth of the Negro Past;* and Dena J. Epstein, *Sinful Tunes and Spirituals.* The best firsthand account of New Orleans funeral customs is Jelly Roll Morton's colorful and thorough evocation of them in his 1938 Library of Congress recordings for Alan Lomax. These are now available again through an Australian company, Swaggie: *Jelly Roll Morton: The Library of Congress Recordings.* Volume 5 (Swaggie S1315) contains the main portion on funeral customs. See also Alan Lomax, *Mister Jelly Roll.*

Acknowledgments

Acknowledgments are always a pleasure to make, since without the support and advice of friends few of us could sustain ourselves through the solitary stretches that go into the making of books. Your friends, as Gary Snyder has observed, are your creative context. In the acknowledgments that follow I wish merely to attempt a sort of public and necessarily partial repayment of the many kindnesses freely given me through the years. I do not intend to implicate anyone named herein in whatever errors or sins may lurk in my text.

First, then, to those artists who welcomed me into their homes and who patiently endured my questions: Danny Barker, the late Oscar (Chicken) Henry, Willie Humphrey, Louis Keppard, Louis Nelson, Max Roach, and Archie Shepp. Then to those associated with Preservation Hall who have done so much to make my visits to New Orleans both productive and enjoyable: Bill Russell, Chris Botsford, Jane Botsford, and especially Allan and Sandra Jaffe. To Frank and Doris Quinn for hours of good New Orleans talk and music. For special kindnesses thanks to New Orleans historian Donald Marquis and to the late Dr. Edmund Souchon, historian and banjoist, who opened doors for me on my first trip to New Orleans; John Hicks, Glenn Sheller, Paul A. Larson, Frances F. Adams, the late Ivan Alexander, Anne C. Rymer, Thomas H. Watkins, Elizabeth Swanson, and the late Pearl Robinson. Michael S. Harper, Bill Hasson, Thomas Berger, Max Roach, and Archie Shepp read portions of the text and were generous with their advice. Elise R. Turner read all of it—in all its forms; her suggestions have been crucial. My editor Barbara Burn believed in this book almost as long and as staunchly as I have, nor is this the first time she has so supported me. Finally, special debts to the late Jim Robinson for reasons that are apparent herein, and to Dick Whitsell, wherever in this world he may be. It was he who first taught me how to listen to this music, and so I owe him a lot for all the subsequent hours of enjoyment I've had through the years since we were kids together in south Chicago.

Index